Presented to

Adrian Levack

From

Uncle Victor   Christmas / 99

Acknowledgments:

We wish to thank the following for their great contributions and encouragement in making the Word & Song Bible come to life.

Design by Bill Farrar
Artwork Coordinated by Jim Leist & Creative Studios
Illustrations by Tim O'Connor
Cover Design by Ed Maksimowicz
Engineered by Randy Moore and Ron Kingery
Music Typeset by Jerry Carraway
Musical Arrangements by Stephen Elkins and Jeff Lippencott
Edited by Gail Rothwell, Pamela Ufen, Rose Walls, and Cindy Elkins
For Sharing the Vision: Dee Ann Grand and Bucky Rosenbaum
Published by Ken Stephens
Sound Effects by David Hoffner
Narrations by Emily Elkins, Matthew Oxley, Allie Smith,
       Jonathan Durham, and Brandon Conger

Character Voices (in alphabetical order): Steve Camp, Steve & Annie Chapman, Roy Clark, Eric Falk, Rev. Jerry Falwell, Keith Fletcher, Dr. Paul & Tammy Gentuso, Dee Ann Grand, Steve Green, Larnelle Harris, Max Lucado, Kohry Miller, Dr. Lloyd Ogilvie, Daniel Palma, Twila Paris, Melissa Riddle, Dr. Adrian Rogers, Mr. George Beverly Shea, Kay DeKalb Smith, Rebecca St. James, Rick & Molly Stewart, Rhonda Stewart, Dean Stone, Joni Eareckson Tada, Reggie White, and Dave Wortman

Wonder Kids Choir: Rebecca Cathey, Teri Deel, Emily Elkins, Emily Estes, Laurie Evans, Tiffani Goddard, Tasha Goddard, Lisa Harper, Amy Lawrence, Stephanie Lippencott, Lindsay McAdams, Emily Walker, and Erin Williams

Crowd noises supplied by the Celebration Choir of The Donelson Fellowship in Nashville, Tennessee; Pastor Robert Morgan

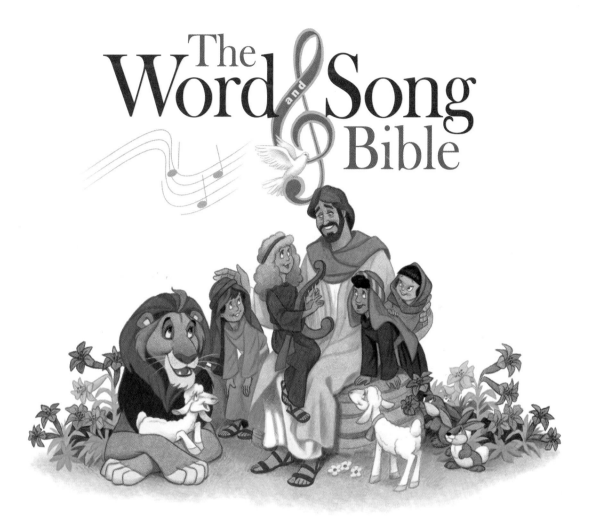

The Word & Song Bible

Stephen Elkins
AUTHOR

Tim O'Connor
ILLUSTRATIONS

BROADMAN
&HOLMAN
PUBLISHERS

NASHVILLE, TENNESSEE

Published in 1999 by
Broadman & Holman Publishers
Nashville, Tennessee

ISBN 0-8054-1689-7

Scripture quotations on pages 1, 8, 13, 21, 30, 35, 50, 55, 94, 108, 110, 113, 126, 131, 143, 149, 170, 173, 180, 189, 199, 202, 211, 219, 224, 234, 238, 240, 246, 248, 254, 256, 258, 285, 296, 299, 301, 311, 316, 350, 378, 380, 384, 387, 390, 393, 396, 399, 405, 407, 410, 414, 417, 420, 422, 424, 426 are from the Holy Bible, New International Version, copyright © 1973, 1978, 1984 by International Bible Society.

Scripture quotations on pages 73, 118, 156, 163, 204, 215, 231, 260, 275, 327, 347, 366, 375, 401, 403, 404, 428 are from the New American Standard Bible, © the Lockman Foundation, 1960, 1962, 1963, 1968, 1971, 1972, 1973, 1975, 1977; used by permission.

All other Scripture quotations are from the *King James Version*.

Library of Congress Cataloging-in-Publication Data

   Elkins, Stephen.
      The word and song Bible / Stephen Elkins ; illustrated by Tim O'Connor.
      p. cm.
   ISBN 0-8054-1689-7
    1. Bible stories, English. 2. Sacred songs Juvenile. [1. Bible stories.
   2. Sacred songs.] I. O'Connor, Tim, ill. II. Title. III. Title: Word
     and song.
     BS551.2 .E39   1999
     220.9'505--dc21   99-30344
                                                    CIP

1 2 3 4 5 03 02 01 00 99

About This Book

This *Word & Song Bible* presents a new world of exciting Bible adventure never before available to your child.

As concerned parents, teachers, friends, and advocates of children, we know it can be challenging competing for a child's attention with so much "entertainment" available. In *Word & Song* we have brought together some of the world's finest writers, authors, Christian educators, illustrators, designers, teachers, preachers, and musicians to create an experience we know your child will love reading (and listening to) for years to come.

Entertaining, yes ... But also INNER-TRAINING!

Over 300 exciting illustrations by Tim O'Connor bring the Bible characters and stories to life. As children read these powerful stories (at least one from each book of the Bible) and sing these inspiring scripture songs, we trust God will plant the seeds of life in their hearts.

You'll thrill to hear your child begin memorizing many precious Bible verses reinforced in *Word & Song*. The color-coded pages make it easy for your child to locate their favorite story or song. We know the reading and singing of God's Word will make a difference in the life of your child.

Dedication

This book is dedicated to all children of the 21st century. May you grow in grace and in the knowledge of our Lord and Savior Jesus Christ.

Stephen Elkins

Stephen Elkins, author of *The Word & Song Bible*
President and founder of Wonder Workshop, Nashville, Tennessee.

TABLE OF CONTENTS

THE OLD TESTAMENT STORIES

THE NEW TESTAMENT STORIES

"*The Lord is my shepherd*
I shall not want."

The OLD TESTAMENT

GENESIS

IN THE BEGINNING

Genesis 1:1 In the beginning God created the heavens and the earth.

In the beginning God created the heavens and the earth. Now the earth had no shape or form, and darkness covered the waters. And the Spirit of God was present, passing over the waters.

And God said, "Let there be light." And there was light! God saw that the light was good, and He separated the light from the dark. He called the light "day" and the darkness "night." So ended the first day of creation.

Then God said, "Let there be a visible arching sky that separates the waters." So God made the sky to separate the waters under it from the waters above it.

And everything that God spoke was accomplished in the power of His word. And so ended the second day of creation.

And God said, "Let the waters under the sky be gathered in one place and let dry land appear." And it was so. God called the dry land "earth" and the gathered waters "seas." And God saw it was good.

Then God made every kind of plant and tree, and God saw that it was good. And so ended the third day of creation.

And then with His word,
God created two great lights ... the sun to shine in the day,
and the moon to brighten the night. He also made millions
of stars. God set them in the heavens to give light to the
earth. And God saw that it was good. So ended the fourth
day of creation.

And God said, "Let the waters be filled with living creatures, and let birds fly through the skies." So God made creatures of every kind that live in the sea and every winged bird that soars above.

And God saw that it was good and He blessed them. And so ended the fifth day of God's marvelous creation.

And God said, "Let the earth produce wild animals, livestock, and all other creatures that walk or creep upon the ground."

Then God said, "Let us make man in our image and let them rule over all creation." So God created man in His own image; male and female He created them. God blessed them and saw that all He had made was good. And so ended the sixth day.

God had finished His work; so on the seventh day He rested.

Affirmation: I am a very special creation of God and He loves me.

In The Beginning

In the beginning God created the heavens and the earth. (Genesis 1:1)

Gen-e-sis,(Gen-e-sis) Verse one, one (Verse one, one)

In the be-gin-ning God cre-a-ted

the hea-vens and the earth. Day

one He made the light;

dark-ness did a-bound. He

called it day and by the way no

earth was spin-ning 'round.

Verse II: Day two, He made the waters, it's enough to laugh. I'm reminded ev'rytime I have to take a bath.

Verse III: Day three, guess what He made? Sailors shout hurray! The seven seas all came to be, on that special day.

Verse IV: Day four, He made the stars shine, the sun and moon above. In heaven's sky on starry nights, I see our Father's love.

Verse V: Day five, He made the sparrows, and every bird that flies. And all the creatures in the sea, God made them on day five.

Verse VI: Day six He made the animals, both big and small you see. And on that day Hip Hip Hooray! God made Adam and Eve.

ADAM AND EVE

Genesis 1:27 (And) God created man in his image,... male and female he created them.

The Lord God used the dust of the ground to create Adam, the first man. When God breathed His breath of life into Adam's nose, he became a living soul.

The Lord placed Adam in a beautiful garden called Eden. It was a perfect home. Adam was given the special job of taking care of all God had made.

Then the Lord said to Adam, "You may eat the fruit from any tree in the garden except one. Do not eat from that tree." And God warned Adam that if he disobeyed and ate the fruit, he would die.

So Adam did the things God asked him to do.

Then the Lord said, "It is not good for Adam to be alone. I will make him a helper and friend." So the Lord caused Adam to fall asleep. God then removed one of Adam's ribs and from it He made a woman.

God brought the woman to Adam and he was very pleased. Together Adam and Eve took care of the garden and worshiped God.

Now the Lord created every beast of the field and every bird in the sky and brought them to Adam one by one. Adam gave each one of them a name.

He gave names to all the cattle, to the birds of the air, and to every beast of the field.

Affirmation: What a wonderful God we serve.

The Reason He Made Me

(And) God created man in his image,...
male and female he created them. (Genesis 1:27)

And God cre-a-ted man in His im-age.

Male and fe-male He cre-a-ted them. And

God cre-a-ted all for His glo-ry. That's the

rea-son all cre-a-tion is prais-ing Him. Oh,

Fa-ther God, I am stand-ing in Your light. Pray

all the world will see. May

all I do glor-i-fy Your Name. That's the

rea - son You made me.

A BAD CHOICE

Genesis 3:19 By the sweat of your brow you will eat your food.

Now there appeared in the garden one day a serpent who had come to tempt Adam and Eve. He was very clever.

One day he found Eve alone in the garden near the forbidden tree and he spoke, "Did God really say not to eat from every tree in the garden?"

13

Eve was startled and said to the serpent, "We may eat the fruit of every tree in the garden except this one. For God has warned us. He said do not eat this fruit or even touch it or we will die."

"You will not die!" said the serpent. "God knows that if you eat the fruit of this tree, you'll be just like Him!"

"Your eyes will be opened and you'll know about good and evil, and you'll be just as powerful as He is!"

Eve then gazed back upon the forbidden fruit. She remembered God's warning, but the serpent's words did seem to make sense. She could see with her own eyes that this fruit looked as ripe and sweet as any in the garden.

"This fruit looks good. It probably tastes good too. And wisdom is something everyone needs! The serpent is right," she thought. "God doesn't want us to be wise!"

So Eve took the fruit and ate it. Soon, Adam came by and she gave the fruit to her husband. He ate it also.

Adam and Eve had sinned against God.

Soon they heard the voice of the Lord as He walked through the garden. "Adam, where are you?" He called.

Adam answered, "We were hiding, Lord, because we were naked and afraid."
Then God said, "Adam, have you eaten from the tree that I warned you not to?"

Adam answered, "The woman you made to be my helper, she gave me the fruit and I did eat."

Then the Lord said to the woman, "What have you done?"

"The serpent confused me, Lord. He told me I would not die and that we could be gods too!" Adam and Eve were afraid and ashamed of what they had done.

Then God said to the serpent, "I curse you this day for what you have done. You will crawl on your belly all the days of your life."

The serpent fell silent on the ground and slithered away.

To Adam the Lord said, "Because you disobeyed Me, you shall work very hard for your daily bread. The ground will be full of thorns and thistles."

The Lord made them clothes to wear and sent them out of the garden of Eden, never to return again. Behind them He placed an angel with a flaming sword to guard the entrance to Eden.

Affirmation: I will seek to obey the Lord.

A Bad Choice

By the sweat of your brow you will eat your food. (Genesis 3:19)

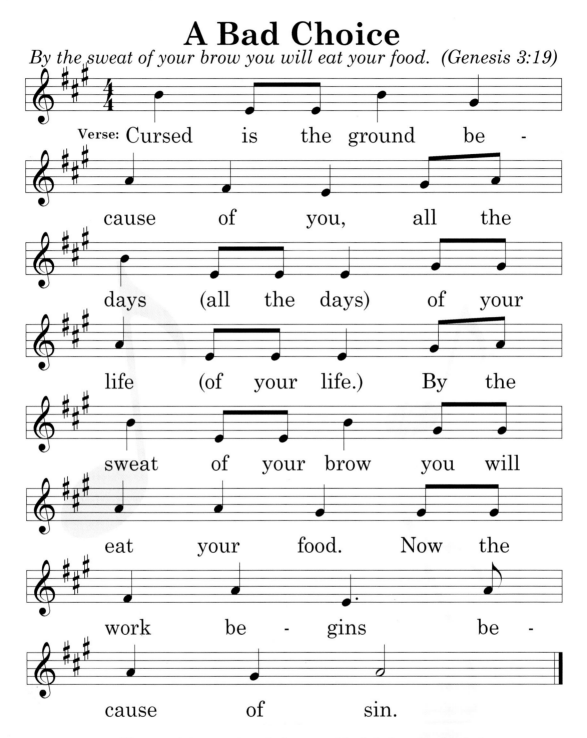

Verse: Cursed is the ground be - cause of you, all the days (all the days) of your life (of your life.) By the sweat of your brow you will eat your food. Now the work be - gins be - cause of sin.

Chorus: Adam made a choice, a real bad choice. He decided he would disobey. Eve made a choice, a real bad choice; then, the world would never be the same.

NOAH'S ARK

Genesis 9:13, 15 I have set my rainbow in the clouds and it will be a sign of the covenant (my promise). Never again will the waters become a flood.

Many years had passed since the day Adam and Eve were forced to leave the garden of Eden. The world was full of people who had become very wicked. They never prayed or thought about their heavenly Father. God's heart became full of pain and He was sorry He had ever created them. So the Lord said, "I will destroy these people whom I have created."

But there was a man named Noah who loved the Lord with all his heart. When everyone else had become selfish and mean, Noah and his family walked with the Lord.

God was pleased with Noah and said, "I am going to send a great flood upon the earth to destroy every living thing. Only you and your family will be saved."

God told Noah to build a large boat, called an ark, out of gopher wood. The ark would have many rooms and a roof over the top to keep out the water.

The Lord said this ark should be 450 feet long, 75 feet wide and 45 feet tall, and have 3 decks. Now we're going to bring two of every kind of bird and beast, male and female, into this ark. Noah did all that God had asked him to do.

So Noah, together with his three sons Shem, Ham, and Japheth, and his wife and his son's wives, built the ark. They brought plenty of food aboard for themselves and the animals to eat.

Soon, the animals came to Noah and were loaded into the ark two by two. Then God said to Noah, "Go into the ark, for it will rain in seven days." Noah did all the Lord commanded.

Seven days soon passed. The skies darkened, the thunder crashed, and the rain began to fall. With two of every living creature aboard, God shut the door on Noah and his family. It rained for forty days and forty nights. The waters rose higher and higher floating the ark high above the earth. Every living thing perished.
Only Noah and those with him in the ark were left.

The earth was flooded for 150 days. But God's watchcare was upon Noah and his family. God sent a warm heavenly breeze to dry the earth. Soon, the ark came to rest in the mountains of Ararat. Noah waited 40 days before he opened the window. He sent out a raven, but there was no dry place for the bird to land.

Then he sent out a dove, but the dove could find no dry place and returned to the ark. Noah waited seven more days before sending the dove out again. This time the dove returned with an olive leaf in its beak ... a sign that there was dry land. Noah waited seven more days and again sent the dove out, but this time the dove did not return.

Then God said to Noah, "Come out of the ark with your wife and your sons and their wives and all the animals." Noah was thankful God had saved his family, so he built an altar to please the Lord. "Thank you Lord for saving my family. You are a wonderful God." God made a promise never again to destroy the world with flood waters. As a sign of His promise, He set a beautiful rainbow in the sky.

Affirmation: I will trust God's promises.

Noah's Arky, Arky

I have set my rainbow in the clouds . . . as a sign of the covenant (promise). Never again will the waters become a flood. (Genesis 9:13)

The Lord said to No - ah, "There's

gon - na be a flood - y, flood - y,

Lord said to No - ah, "There's

gon - na be a flood - y, flood - y,

Get those child - ren

(clap) out of the mud - dy, mud - dy,

Child-ren of the Lord.

Verse II: It rained and poured for forty long daizies, daizies. (Repeat) Nearly drove those animals crazy, crazy. Children of the Lord.

Verse III: I have set my rainbow in the cloudies, cloudies. (Repeat) As a sign of (clap) my promise "vow-deed", "vow-deed". Children of the Lord.

Verse IV: Never again will waters become floody, floody. (Repeat) To destroy all (clap) life in the muddy, muddy. Children of the Lord.

ABRAHAM AND SARAH'S SURPRISE

Genesis 18:14 Is anything too hard for the Lord (to do)?

Noah's oldest son, Shem, had hundreds of descendants born many years later. One was named Abram. Abram was a righteous man who married a beautiful woman named Sarai. One day the Lord spoke to Abram and said, "Leave your country, your family, and neighbors and go to a land I will show you. There I will bless you and make you into a great nation."

So Abram obeyed the Lord and set out on a journey with his wife Sarai and his nephew, Lot. One night the Lord appeared to Abram and said, "Look up at the night sky and count the stars. One day your family shall number more than that!" Abram was very puzzled by what the Lord had said for he and Sarai were growing old and had no children.

When Abram was 99 years old, the Lord appeared to him again and said, "Abram, I make this promise to you. You will be called the father of many nations, and you shall be called Abraham and your wife shall be called Sarah.

For I will bless her with a son and you will call his name Isaac. And I will give to you and your children this land. I will care for you and be your God." Abraham laughed and said, "How can a son be born to people our age?"

Sarah overheard what the Lord had said to her husband and she, too, laughed and laughed! "How can this be?" she giggled.

But the Lord heard her laughter and said, "Is anything too hard for the Lord? I will return next year and you, Sarah, will have a son."

When Abraham was 100 years old, Sarah had a little baby boy named Isaac, just as God had promised.

Affirmation: There is nothing too hard for the Lord to do!

Isaac's Lullaby

Is anything too hard for the Lord (to do)? (Genesis 18:14)

Lul - la - by and good - night. Go to
sleep lit - tle I - saac. Lul-la - by and good -
night, God is watch-ing o'er us all. Is an-y-
thing too hard for the Lord to
do? Fear not, He'll keep you safe the
whole night through.

Verse II: Lullaby and goodnight, go to sleep little baby. Lullaby and goodnight, go
to sleep my little child. If God wills, thou shalt wake when the morning does
break. If God wills, thou shalt wake when the morning does break.

ABRAHAM OBEYED

Genesis 22:18 Through your offspring (children) all nations on earth will be blessed.

Abraham and Sarah loved their son Isaac very much. He was living proof that God had been faithful to them and would keep His promises.

Several years had now passed and Sarah's little baby Isaac had grown to be a young boy. God decided He would test Abraham. The Lord said, "Abraham, take your son ... your only son Isaac, whom you love, and go to the land called Moriah. Sacrifice him there as an offering to Me."

Abraham's heart was broken to think that Isaac must die, but he trusted God to do the right thing. Early the next morning Abraham arose and saddled his donkey. Then he and Isaac and two servants set out for Moriah.

After three days' journey, they could see the place in the distance. Abraham said to his servants, "Stay here with the donkey while Isaac and I go there to worship."

Together Abraham and Isaac climbed the steep pathway toward the place the Lord was showing them. Abraham could not speak. His heart was breaking.

Finally, Isaac spoke up and said, "Father?" "Yes, my son?" Abraham answered. "The fire and wood are here. But where is the lamb for the sacrifice?" Abraham answered, "God will provide the lamb." And they walked on.

When they finally reached the place, Abraham built an altar and set the wood on it. Then he bound his son Isaac and laid him on the altar.

Abraham looked into heaven and slowly raised his knife to slay his son. Then an angel called out, "Abraham! Do not lay a hand on the boy. Now I know that you fear God because you have offered your son, your only son, as a sacrifice."

Suddenly, Abraham heard the sound of a ram bleating. It was caught by its horns in a nearby thicket.

Abraham cut Isaac loose, took the ram, and sacrificed it unto the Lord. So Abraham called that place "The Lord will Provide."

Then the angel of the Lord called to Abraham a second time. "Abraham, because you have done this and have not withheld your only son, you and your family will be blessed above all people."

Affirmation:
Lord, make me a
blessing to others!

Old Father Abraham

Through your offspring (children) all nations
on earth will be blessed. (Genesis 22:18)

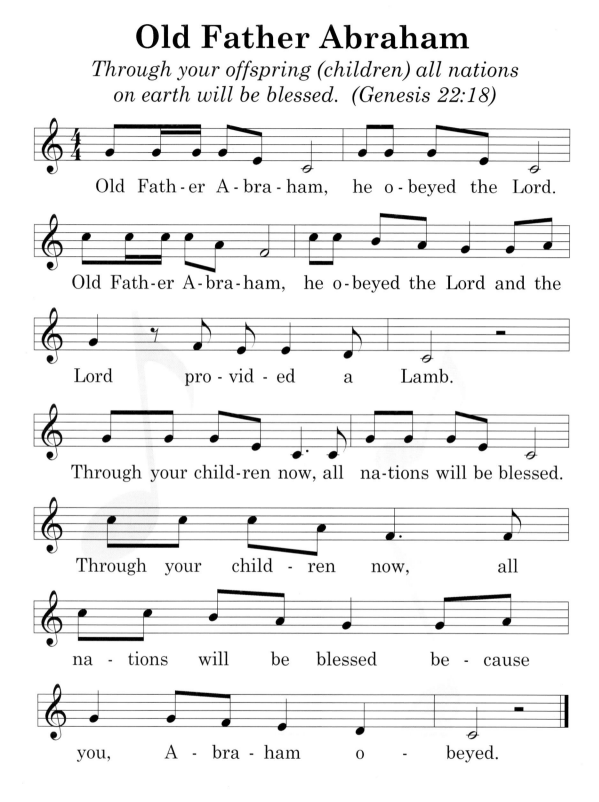

Old Fath-er A-bra-ham, he o-beyed the Lord.

Old Fath-er A-bra-ham, he o-beyed the Lord and the

Lord pro-vid-ed a Lamb.

Through your child-ren now, all na-tions will be blessed.

Through your child - ren now, all

na - tions will be blessed be - cause

you, A - bra - ham o - beyed.

ESAU AND JACOB:
THE TROUBLE WITH TWINS   *Genesis 25-27*

Now Isaac loved the Lord and grew to be a great man of God. At age 40, he married a woman named Rebekah. Like Abraham and Sarah, they prayed that God would bless them with a child.

When Isaac was 60 years old, the Lord answered their prayers with a double blessing ... Rebekah was going to have twins! Even before the babies were born, Rebekah felt them kicking and fighting each other. "Why is this happening?" she asked the Lord.

The Lord answered and said, "Two nations are inside of you and the two will be separated. One will be stronger than the other; the older brother will serve the younger."

On the day of their birth, Esau, the first-born, was red and hairy. Jacob was fair and smooth and followed with his hand grasping Esau's heel. Just as Rebekah had been told, the two boys were very different.

Esau grew up to be a very
skillful hunter, while Jacob liked to stay close to home.
One day Esau came home weary and tired from a
long day's hunt. Jacob had just finished cooking
some tasty stew. Esau was very hungry when
he said, "Jacob, let me have some of your stew."
Jacob replied, "First, sell me your birthright."
This meant that Jacob, the second born, would have all
the special honors given to the first-born.

Again, Jacob said, "Give me your birthright and I will give you food." Esau, being so tired and with the smell of Jacob's stew tempting him, replied, "I'm about to die anyway. What good is a birthright if you're dead of hunger. You can have it! Now, give me some stew!"

"Swear to me first," Jacob demanded.

So Esau swore before the Lord and gave Jacob his birthright. How foolish he was to sell his birthright for so little!

Many years passed and their father Isaac became very old and blind. Fearing he may die soon, he called for Esau and said, "Take your bow and arrow to the country and bring back some wild game. Prepare a meal just the way I like it and bring it to me. Then I will give you my blessing."

When Rebekah heard what Isaac had said to Esau, she called for Jacob. She told Jacob she had a plan to trick Isaac so that he would be the one to take the food to Isaac and receive the blessing. Jacob was concerned Isaac would know.

He said to his mother, "Esau is hairy and I am not. What if father touches me and finds out I am not Esau? What if he curses me instead of blesses me?"

"The curse will be upon me," Rebekah said. "Now do as I tell you!" Then Jacob dressed in Esau's clothes and with his hands covered with goat skins, took the meal into his father's room.

Jacob said, "The Lord God has given me a successful hunt. Rise and eat and give me your blessing." Isaac said, "Come close so I may touch you to know if you are really Esau." When Isaac touched the hairy goat skin hands and smelled Esau's clothes, he blessed him saying, "May all people bless and serve you. May nations bow down to you." Now Jacob had taken Esau's birthright and blessing.

Just as Jacob left his father's room, in came Esau with the tasty meal he had prepared for his father. "Rise and eat and give me your blessing," Esau said.

"Who are you?" Isaac asked. "I am your first-born son, Esau," he answered. Isaac trembled, "Who was it then that brought me food and received my blessing? For he will be blessed indeed."

When Esau heard his fathers words, he cried, "Bless me, too. Father, bless me, too!" Isaac raised his head and said, "Your brother has deceived me. He has taken your blessing and I have made him lord over you and all his relatives. I can give you nothing."

Esau hated Jacob and said to all, "The day is coming when I will kill Jacob."

Affirmation: I will be a blessing to others!

JACOB'S STAIRWAY TO HEAVEN

Genesis 28:15 (Behold) I am with you and will watch over you.

When Rebekah heard what Esau had said, she sent for Jacob and told him to leave at once. "You must go to my brother Laban's house in Haran. Stay there until Esau's anger is quieted."

Rebekah told her husband that Jacob was going to Haran to find a godly wife. So Isaac blessed him with the blessings of Abraham and sent him on his way.

One evening on the way to Haran, Jacob stopped to rest for the night. He spread his blanket across the ground and used a large stone for a pillow. He fell asleep and dreamed he saw a stairway to heaven. The bottom of the stairway rested on the earth, the top reached to heaven. And the angels of God were climbing up and down the heavenly stairway.

There above the stairway stood Yahweh, our Lord, and He said, "I am the Lord the God of Abraham, your grandfather, and the God of Isaac, your father. I make this promise to you. I will give to you and your children this land where you are now sleeping. All the people on earth will be blessed because of you and your family. I will watch over you and no matter where you go, I will be with you."

Jacob woke
up frightened.
"Surely the presence
of the Lord is in this
place and I didn't know it,"
he said. So early the next morning Jacob
arose and took his stone pillow and poured
oil over it and set it as a reminder
to the whole world that God had been there.

Then Jacob made a promise to God.
"If God will watch over me on this
journey and I return safely to my father's
house, then Yahweh the Lord will be
my God and I will give Him a tenth of all I may own."

Affirmation: I know the Lord is watching over me!

We Are Climbing Jacob's Ladder

*(Behold) I am with you and will watch
over you.   (Genesis 28:15)*

We are climb-ing Ja-cob's lad-der. We are climb-ing

Jac-ob's lad-der. We are climb-ing Jac-ob's lad-der,

Sold-iers of the Cross. Be - hold I am with you and

will watch o'er you. Be - hold I am with you and

will watch o'er you. Be - hold I am with you and

will watch o'er you, Sold-iers of the Cross.

Verse III: Every round goes higher, higher.
Every round goes higher, higher. Every round
goes higher, higher. Soldiers of the Cross.

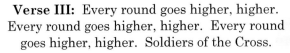

54

JOSEPH: GOD PUT A DREAM IN MY HEART

Genesis 37:5 Joseph had a dream, and when he told it to his brothers, they hated him.

Some years later, Jacob married and had twelve sons. He settled in a place called Canaanland where his sons tended flocks of sheep.

Now Jacob had a favorite son named Joseph who was born when Jacob was very old. To show his great love, Jacob made Joseph a coat of many colors. Many times Joseph would come to his father and tell him the bad things his brothers were doing. This made his brothers very angry and jealous.

Joseph's brothers hated him for this and could not speak a kind word to him. One night the Lord sent Joseph a very special dream.

The next morning Joseph told his brothers all about it. He said, "We were in the fields tying bundles of grain together when suddenly my bundle rose up and stood tall while your bundles gathered around mine and bowed down to it."

"Do you think you will someday rule over us?" his brothers said. And they hated him even more.

Then Joseph had a second dream. He said to his brothers, "This time the sun, the moon, and eleven stars were bowing down to me." When he told the dream to his father, Jacob was very unhappy. "Do you believe that your mother, and I, and your eleven brothers will bow down before you?"

One day Jacob said to Joseph, "Your brothers are tending to our flocks near Shechem. Go to them and make sure all is well."

Joseph obeyed his father and soon found his brothers on a hillside. But his brothers had seen Joseph's coat of many colors from a distance, and before Joseph reached them, they plotted to kill him.

"Here comes the dreamer," they said. "Let's kill him and throw him into one of these empty water holes and say a wild animal attacked and killed him. That will put an end to his dreams!"

When the oldest brother Reuben heard their plan, he stopped it. "Do not kill him. Throw him into the pit, but do not harm him."

When Joseph saw his brothers, he ran to them. Suddenly, to his surprise, they all jumped on him and began tearing his coat of many colors from his back. They tied him up and threw him into an empty water hole.

As they sat to eat, a caravan bound for Egypt passed by. Judah spoke, "Why don't we sell Joseph to these merchants? Then we'll be rid of him forever!"

Joseph was sold as a slave to the merchants for twenty pieces of silver. When Reuben found out what they had done, he said, "How can we face our father having done this?"

They decided to kill a young goat and dip Joseph's coat in the blood. They took the coat to their father and said, "Father we found this coat on our journey back home. Is it Joseph's?"

Jacob knew it was Joseph's coat and cried out, "It is Joseph's coat! Some wild animal has killed my son! He must have been torn to pieces."

Then Jacob tore his clothes and wept bitterly. No one was able to comfort him. Meanwhile, Joseph was on his way to Egypt.

Affirmation: I will not be jealous of others!

Joseph Had A Coat Of Many Colors

Joseph had a dream, and when he told it to his brothers, they hated him. (Genesis 37:5)

JOSEPH: FROM PRISON TO A PALACE
Genesis 39-41

When the merchant caravan reached Egypt, Joseph was sold to an Egyptian named Potiphar who worked for the king as captain of the guard. Being an honorable man, Joseph soon became Potiphar's most trusted servant. Joseph even lived in Potiphar's house and was put in charge of all he owned.

Potiphar's wife became angry with Joseph because he would not disobey the law of the Lord. She said things about Joseph that were not true. Because of her lies, Potiphar had Joseph put in prison.

Sometime later the king's baker and servant were also put into the same prison. Joseph took care of them. While they were there, each one had a dream which troubled them greatly. Joseph noticed their sad faces and asked, "Why are you so sad?"

"Last night we both had the strangest dreams and we don't know what they mean," they said.
"God knows everything," answered Joseph. "With His help, perhaps I can explain the dreams to you."

The king's servant spoke first. "I saw a vine with three branches which budded and blossomed into ripe grapes.

The king's cup was in my hand, so I squeezed the grapes into the cup and put the cup into the king's hand."

Then Joseph explained, "The three branches are three days. In three days the king will call for you and you will once again be his chief servant. When this happens, please mention me to the king and get me out of this prison for I have done nothing wrong."

The chief baker spoke up. "In my dream, on my head were three wicker baskets. The top basket was full of bread for the king, but the birds were pecking the bread to pieces."

Then Joseph said, "The three baskets are three days. In three days the king will have your head cut off and hang you on a tree, and the birds will eat your flesh."

Everything happened the way Joseph said it would. The servant was freed, but the baker was killed.

Two years passed, and the king had a troubling dream. He called the wisest men of Egypt to explain it, but they could not

Then the king's servant remembered Joseph and how Joseph had explained his dream while he was in prison. He spoke to the king. "There was a Hebrew slave named Joseph I met in prison who once explained the meaning of my dreams to me. All that he said came to pass. Perhaps he will know the meaning of your dream."

The king sent for Joseph and said to him, "I am told that you can explain the meaning of my dreams ... is this true?" Joseph answered, "I cannot, but my God can. He will give you the meaning of your dreams."

The king told Joseph of his dream.

"I was standing by the Nile River when I saw seven fat cows come out of the water. Then seven skinny cows came out of the water. Then the skinny cows ate up the fat cows, but no one could tell they had eaten. Then I woke up."

"Later, I had a second dream where I saw seven ripe and healthy heads of grain growing on a single stalk. There sprang up seven more heads of grain, but these were withered and thin.

Then, the seven thin heads of grain swallowed up the seven healthy heads. Is your God able to tell me the meaning of these dreams?"

Joseph answered, "God has indeed made known to you what He is about to do. The dreams are one and the same."

"The seven fat cows and the seven healthy heads of grain are seven years. The seven skinny cows and the seven withered heads of grain are also seven years. God has twice shown you that there will be seven years of plentiful food followed by seven years of famine and starvation. You should put a wise man in charge of saving up a part of the harvest in the good years to be eaten in the bad years."

The king thought Joseph's idea was very good, so he made Joseph second in command over Egypt to carry out the task of storing food for the coming famine.

Affirmation: I will do the right thing, for God is watching!

JOSEPH: FATHER AND SON REUNION

Genesis 50:19-20 Do not be afraid ... you meant evil against me, but God meant it for good,... to (save) many people.

Just as Pharaoh's dream had foretold, there were seven years of plenty. Joseph gathered a portion of the grain and stored it in the cities.

Then came the seven years of famine. The people cried out to Pharaoh for food.

Joseph then opened the storehouses of grain and there was plenty of food.

In Canaan, where Joseph's father and brothers lived, there was very little food. "We must not delay," Jacob told his sons. "I have heard there is plenty of food in Egypt. Go there to buy grain." So ten of Jacob's sons left for Egypt. Benjamin, the youngest son, stayed with his father.

When the ten brothers arrived in Egypt, they were presented to Joseph. They bowed down to him with their faces to the ground.

Joseph knew they were his brothers, but he pretended not to know them and spoke harshly to them. "Where do you come from?" he asked.

"From Canaan," they replied. "We've come to buy grain." Then Joseph remembered the dreams he had about them.

"You are spies," Joseph said.

"No, my lord, we are the twelve sons of Jacob. The youngest is with him now, and we do not know where our other brother is."

"You are spies!" Joseph repeated, "and you will be tested!"

Then he put them in prison.

Three days later Joseph said, "One of you must stay here in this prison. The rest of you will return to your father's house.

Take this food to your starving family, but you must bring your youngest brother back to me. Then I will know you are telling the truth, and you will not die. Now, go!" Then Joseph had his brother Simeon bound before their eyes.

Secretly, Joseph ordered his servants to fill their bags with grain and to put the money they had used for payment back in their bags. After this was done, the nine brothers started home.

Evening came and Joseph's brothers stopped to rest for the night. As they opened their grain sacks to feed the donkeys, they were frightened to find their own money. "What is God doing to us?" they asked. And they were afraid.

Soon, they arrived in Canaan and they told their father the things that had happened. "We must return to Egypt with Benjamin," they said. "No!" Jacob shouted. "Joseph and Simeon are gone and I will not allow Benjamin to go."

But when Jacob and his family had eaten all the grain, he knew that Benjamin would have to return with his brothers to Egypt to buy more grain if they were to survive. They prayed that God would be with them.

This time, they hurried down to Egypt taking with them special gifts for Governor Joseph. When Joseph saw them coming with his brother Benjamin, he said, "Servants, prepare a meal for these men." Then he left.

Joseph's brothers were afraid. They thought they might be put in prison for stealing, so they tried to return the money they had found in their bags to Joseph's servant.

But the servant said, "Do not be afraid. The money you found was a gift from God."

Joseph had Simeon brought to them, and when he returned they gave him the gifts they had brought. Again, they bowed down before Joseph. As Joseph spoke to Benjamin, his heart was deeply moved with love. But Joseph still did not tell them who he was.

When the meal ended, Joseph ordered his servants to fill their grain bags to overflowing and again to put each man's silver in their bags. Then he said, "Be sure to put my silver cup in Benjamin's sack." His servants obeyed.

When morning came, his brothers left for Canaan with the bags of grain. Shortly thereafter, Joseph sent his servant after them and he said, "My master was good to you. Why have you repaid him with evil and stolen his silver cup?"

"We have stolen nothing," the brothers answered. "Search our bags. If you find the silver cup, the owner of that bag will die and we will become your master's slaves." So they each lowered their bags to the ground and opened them. The servant pretended to search each bag and found the silver cup in Benjamin's bag, right where he had put it. The brothers were surprised and could not believe it! They loaded their donkeys and returned to the city.

They went into Joseph's house and bowed down before him terrified they would be put to death. Judah spoke, "God is punishing us for a terrible thing we did long ago. Now we are your slaves and Benjamin is at your mercy."

But Joseph said, "I cannot do such a thing to you. Only the one who has stolen my cup will stay here. The rest of you must go back to your father in peace."

Judah walked closer to Joseph and said, "My lord, if Benjamin remains here, I am certain our father will die of a broken heart. For he especially loves Benjamin as he did our other brother. Please take me in his place and let Benjamin return to our father."

When Joseph heard this, he could no longer hold back the tears.

"I am Joseph!" he shouted. "I am Joseph, the brother you sold into slavery." His brothers were frightened and could not believe it was him.

Then Joseph said, "Come close to me, and do not be angry with yourselves. For it was God who sent me here ahead of you to save you and your children from the famine. You intended to harm me, but God intended it for good."

Joseph then sent for his father Jacob. When Jacob arrived in Egypt, Joseph embraced him. Jacob said, "Now I can die in peace, for I have seen my son." Jacob and all of his family moved to Egypt where they lived for many years.

Affirmation:
Our God is an awesome God!

Awesome God

Do not be afraid ... you meant evil against me, but God meant it for good,... to (save) many people. (Genesis 50: 19-20)

Do not be a-fraid, do not be a-fraid, our

God is an awe - some God. Though you

meant e - vil a - gainst me to - day, our

God is an awe - some God.

God meant it for good to

save ma - ny peo - ple.

God meant it for good. Our

God is an awe - some God.

EXODUS BABY MOSES

Exodus 2

Many years later, after Joseph and all his brothers had died, Pharaoh was the new king of Egypt. He feared the children of Jacob, now called Israelites. "The Israelites are growing too strong," he said. "If there is a war, they may fight against us and defeat us."

To keep this from happening, he made the Israelites into slaves and put Egyptian masters over them. They were forced to work very hard making bricks and mortar.

Pharaoh used the bricks to build great cities. But no matter how unkind the Egyptian slave masters were, or how hard their work became, the Israelites continued to grow in number.

Pharaoh became so angry he passed a cruel law ordering every baby boy born to an Israelite family to be drowned in the Nile River.

Now it happened that a baby boy was born to an Israelite family. Fearing Pharaoh's decree, the mother hid the baby for months. But when he began to cry and move about, she had to do something to save him. She decided to make a large basket out of the reeds that grew near the river. She sealed it with sticky tar so it would float.

Then she put the baby in the basket and set it among the reeds along the riverbank. His sister, Miriam, stood at a distance to watch over the baby.

That evening, Pharaoh's daughter went down to the river to bathe. It was then she noticed the strange basket floating among the reeds. "Fetch that basket," she said to her servant girl. When she opened the basket and saw the little baby boy, she loved him.

Then Miriam came forth and said, "Would you like for me to get an Israelite woman to take care of the baby?" "Yes, I would," said the princess.

So Miriam ran back to get her mother and told her the things that had happened. "Take care of this baby and bring him back to me when he is older," the princess said.

When the child grew older, his mother took him to Pharaoh's palace, back to the princess, and he became her son. The princess named him Moses saying, "I drew him out of the water."

Affirmation: God will keep me safe!

WORDS FROM A BURNING BUSH

Exodus 3:15 This is my name forever, the name by which I am to be remembered.

Moses grew up in an Egyptian palace, but he knew he was an Israelite by birth. One day he went out to see how his people were being treated. He saw an Egyptian beating an Israelite worker. Moses had pity on the worker and tried to stop the beating. In anger, Moses killed the slave master and hid his body in the sand.

In time, Pharaoh found out what Moses had done. He declared that Moses must die. So Moses fled to the land of Midian.

One day while Moses was leading his sheep to Horeb, also called "the mountain of God," an angel appeared from within a burning bush.

Moses thought it was very strange that this bush, though on fire, did not burn up. Then God spoke to Moses from within the burning bush. "Moses, Moses," He said. "Here I am," Moses answered. "Do not come any closer. Take off your sandals, for the place you are standing is holy ground. I am the God of Abraham, the God of Isaac, and the God of Jacob." When Moses heard this he was afraid to look at God, so he hid his face.

"I have heard the cries and prayers of My people in Egypt. So go now. I am sending you to Pharaoh to free My people and lead them out of Egypt into a good land, a land flowing with milk and honey." But Moses said to God, "Who am I that I should lead the Israelites out of Egypt?" God answered, "I will be with you."

"Who shall I tell them sent me?" Moses asked. God answered, "I AM that I AM. Tell them I AM sent you."

Moses asked, "What if they do not believe me? What if they will not listen?" Then God commanded Moses to throw down his staff. Moses obeyed and suddenly the staff became a snake. As Moses took hold of the snake, it turned back into a staff.

Then the Lord spoke to Moses again, "If they do not believe you, take some water from the Nile River and pour it on the ground. It will become blood." But Moses did not want to go and spoke again. "O Lord, I don't speak very well, and my speech is slow. Please send someone else."

This angered God and he said, "Your brother Aaron speaks very well. He will go with you. Tell him what to say and he will say it."

So Moses and his brother Aaron left for Egypt.

Affirmation:
I will go where
God sends me!

Moses Where Have You Been

This is my name forever, the name by which
I am to be remembered. (Exodus 3:15)

Verse I: Mos-es, Mos-es where have you been?

Up on the moun-tain top with the Lord a-gain.

Mos-es, Mos-es now we un-der-stand. His

name is Yah-weh: I Am who I Am.

Chorus: This is My name for-ev-er, the

name by which I am to be re-mem-bered.

This is My name for-ev-er. From

age to age it chang-es nev-er.

Verse II: Moses, Moses did your spirit soar? High upon the mountain top, listening to the
Lord? Moses, Moses now we understand. His name is Yahweh: I Am who I Am.

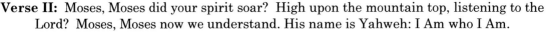

LET MY PEOPLE GO!

Exodus 5-11

Moses and Aaron arrived in Egypt and went to see the Pharaoh. Moses said, "The Lord God of Israel says 'Let My people go, so that they may celebrate their deliverance and worship Me in the desert.'" Pharaoh said to Moses, "I do not believe in your God and I certainly will not obey Him. The slaves are mine and I will not let them go."

Then Pharaoh gave an order to the slave masters. "Do not give the Israelites any more straw for making bricks. Make them gather their own straw after they have finished working. But I want the number of bricks they make each day to be the same." This made their work even harder. Soon, the Israelites were beaten for falling behind in their work. Moses prayed, "O Lord, why have You brought more trouble upon Your people?" Then the Lord answered, "Because of My mighty hand, Pharaoh will let My people go. Tell My people that I am Yahweh, the Lord, and I will bring them out of bondage. They will be free and I will lead them to the land I promised Abraham."

Then the Lord said to Moses, "Go back to Pharaoh and tell him to let My people go! I will harden his heart so that he will not listen to you. But through it all, I will show Egypt that I am the true and living God. I will bring many hardships on them and soon the Israelites will be free."

Moses and Aaron returned to Pharaoh's palace and proclaimed, "The Lord has said, 'Let My people go.' Obey the Lord!" Then Aaron threw down the staff of Moses before Pharaoh and it became a snake. Pharaoh called for his magicians. When they threw down their staffs, they also became snakes. But they were amazed as Aaron's staff swallowed up theirs. But just as the Lord had said, Pharaoh would not listen.

God brought many unpleasant things upon the Egyptian people because Pharaoh would not obey God. First, Aaron dipped Moses' staff into the Nile River and it turned to blood. All of the fish died and the smell was terrible. No one could drink the water.

Seven days later Moses returned to Pharaoh and said, "The Lord says, 'Let My people go.' If you do not, I will fill the land with frogs. They will be in every house, even in your beds." Pharaoh said, "I will not free the people." So Aaron stretched out his hand with the staff, and there were frogs everywhere.

"Moses, pray that these awful frogs go away and I will let the people go," promised Pharaoh. So Moses cried out to God and the frogs went away. But Pharaoh broke his promise and did not let the people go.

"Let my people go!" cried Moses, but Pharaoh would not. So Aaron struck the ground with Moses' staff and tiny little gnats began to bite the Egyptians. Then the Lord sent swarms of flies to plague the Egyptians. They covered the entire land of Egypt, but there were no flies swarming near the Israelites.

"Moses, pray that these flies go away and I will free the people," promised Pharaoh. Moses asked the Lord to remove the flies, and God answered his prayer. But Pharaoh would not let the people go.

"Let my people go!" cried Moses, but Pharaoh would not. So the Lord sent a terrible disease that caused the horses and donkeys and camels, even the cattle and sheep to die. Then painful boils broke out on the Egyptians and their animals.

Then Moses stretched out his staff towards the sky and the Lord sent a terrible storm. There was thunder and lightning, and hailstones falling in the fields causing their crops to be beaten down. "Moses!" cried Pharaoh. "We have had enough! I will let the people go. Now pray that this terrible storm may go away." Moses knew Pharaoh would not keep his word, but to show God's power, he prayed and the stormy weather went away.

Then Moses returned to Pharaoh's palace and said, "How long will you refuse to obey the Lord? Let my people go! If you refuse, locusts will cover the ground so it cannot be seen. And they will eat every green plant left by the hailstones."

"No!" shouted Pharaoh. So Moses stretched out his staff and locusts came and covered the ground until it was black. They ate everything growing in the fields and nothing remained.

Pharaoh again called for Moses. "I have sinned, forgive me. Now pray to your God to take away these deadly locusts."

Moses prayed to the Lord and soon came a strong wind that carried the locusts into the Red Sea. Not a single locust was left anywhere in Egypt. But Pharaoh would not let the children of Israel go.

Then the Lord said, "Stretch out your staff toward the sky so that darkness will cover the land." Moses obeyed. For three days total darkness covered all of Egypt, yet the Israelites had light in their homes. Moses again said to Pharaoh, "The Lord says, 'Let My people go.'"

But Pharaoh was angry and he would not change his mind. "Get out of my sight, Moses, and don't you ever come back here again. If you do, I will kill you!" Then the Lord said to Moses, "I will send one more plague upon Egypt, then Pharaoh will let My people go."

Moses warned Pharaoh of a final plague. "The Lord has said, 'At midnight, I will go throughout Egypt and every first-born child will die. Even your son, Pharaoh, will die. And a great cry will come forth from the people.

Your rulers will bow before me saying, *You and the Israelites must go now.*'" Then Moses left Pharaoh's palace angry that Pharaoh refused to listen to God.

THE PASSOVER

Exodus 12:13 ...and when I see the blood, I will pass over you.

The Lord told Moses and Aaron how to prepare for the last plague. "Tell My people that on the tenth day of this month, each household is to select one perfect lamb. Take care of it for four days and then kill the lamb at twilight. Take some of the lamb's blood and smear it on the sides and top of your doorposts. That night, you are to eat the lamb in haste, for it is the Lord's Passover.

On that night, the Lord will pass through Egypt. But when I see the lamb's blood on your doorposts, I will pass over you. You are to remember this day forever, and celebrate your freedom."

At midnight the death angel came and all the first-born in every household in Egypt died, even Pharaoh's son. But no one died in the Israelite homes with the blood smeared over the door. Pharaoh cried to Moses, "Go! Leave as fast as you can before we all die." The Israelites were free at last.

Affirmation: It is good to obey the Lord!

Pass Over Me

And when I see the blood, I will pass over you. (Exodus 12:13)

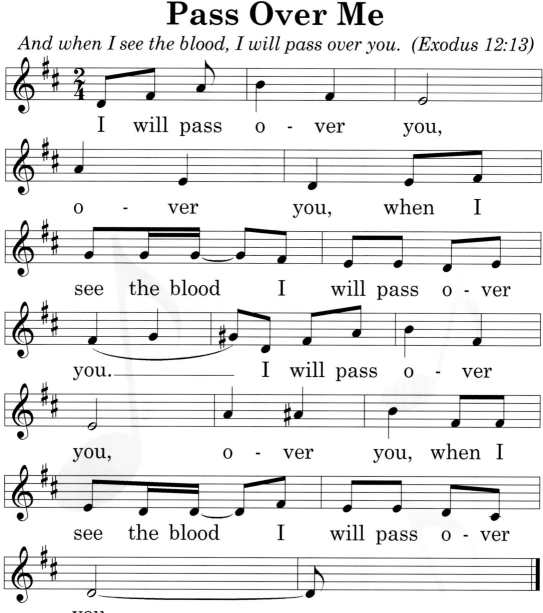

I will pass o - ver you, o - ver you, when I see the blood I will pass o - ver you. I will pass o - ver you, o - ver you, when I see the blood I will pass o - ver you.

Verse I: It's called the Passover and why, you say. While they're in Egypt land there came a plague. But God was there again. That plague passed over them and they were saved by simple faith. On that judgment day when all shall stand before the Lord our God, please understand, if the blood of Jesus Christ is covering your life Heaven will be your home you see.

THE RED SEA MIRACLE

Exodus 14:14   The Lord will fight for you; you need only to be still.

Six hundred thousand men, plus women and children, set off for the promised land. To guide Moses and the Israelites, the Lord sent a huge pillar of clouds to follow during the day, and a great pillar of fire as a guiding light by night.

As soon as the Israelites left Egypt, Pharaoh's heart was quick to change his mind once again. "What have we done? We must capture the Israelites so they can work for us again."

Pharaoh took six hundred of his fastest chariots and an army of soldiers to capture the Israelites. As Moses reached the shores of the Red Sea, the Israelites saw the army coming. They were terrified. "We will die here in the desert," they cried.

Moses shouted, "Stand firm! Do not be afraid. The Lord will fight for you." Then Moses lifted his staff and the seas parted. It was a miracle! The children of Israel walked through the sea with the walls of water all around them.

The Egyptian army followed Moses into the wall of water. But when morning came, the Lord threw the Egyptian army into confusion. The wheels on their chariots broke.

When the Israelites reached the other side, Moses stretched out his staff over the Red Sea. The powerful waters crashed down on top of the Egyptian army. They were defeated. Then the people of Israel put their trust in God.

Affirmation: I serve a God of miracles!

THE JOURNEY

Exodus 20:2 I am the Lord your God, who brought you out of Egypt.

With the Egyptian army defeated by the Lord, the Israelites began their long journey through the wilderness. They were filled with joy and bound for the promised land. The people feared God and trusted Moses, His servant.

The wilderness was a very harsh and dry place, but the Lord provided sweet water to drink. Each morning the Lord rained down bread from heaven called manna. The people gathered it in baskets, enough for each day. It tasted like wafer cookies made with honey!

After three months of travel, the group reached Mount Sinai where they made camp. Then Moses went up the mountain where the Lord spoke to him. The Lord said to tell the people of Israel to obey His rules. Then they would be His special people, a holy nation.

Moses returned to the people and told them what God had said. The people agreed to do all the Lord had commanded.

The Lord said He would
come before the people in
a thick cloud. Everyone would hear
Him speak and always trust Moses. He told Moses to have
the people wash and make themselves clean, for in three
days He would come down to Mount Sinai.

On the morning of the third day, there was thunder and
lightning. Then a thick cloud came over the mountain and
a very loud trumpet sounded. Everyone was afraid.

Then Moses led the people to meet with God at the foot of the mountain. It was smoking like a furnace and the whole mountain shook. Moses called out and God answered.

God called Moses to the top of Mount Sinai and spoke these words, "I am the Lord your God who brought you out of Egypt." Then He gave Moses the Ten Commandments.

THE TEN COMMANDMENTS

1. You shall have no other gods but Me.
2. You shall not worship anything you make with your hands that looks like a creation of Mine.
3. You shall not use the name of the Lord to swear or curse.
4. You shall keep the Sabbath Day holy.
5. Honor your father and your mother.
6. You shall not commit murder.
7. You shall not commit adultery.
8. You shall not steal.
9. You shall not lie.
10. Do not covet, but be content with what you have.

Affirmation: I will obey the Ten Commandments!

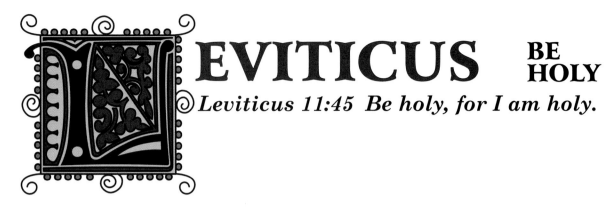

LEVITICUS

BE HOLY

Leviticus 11:45 Be holy, for I am holy.

The children of Israel traveled through the wilderness for forty years. The Lord took care of them, feeding and clothing them all along the way. During this time he taught Moses and the nation of Israel how to worship and obey Him. He said, "Be holy, for I am holy." He taught them to bring five special kinds of offerings or gifts to the Lord.

There were burnt offerings given to the Lord to show forgiveness, grain offerings to show honor and respect, and peace offerings, which were animals without any defects presented to the Lord to show thankfulness.

There were also sin offerings given when someone had broken the law of the Lord without knowing; and the guilt offering was necessary if a person broke the Lord's commandment and caused harm to someone else.

These laws taught the people to live as God commanded and to ask forgiveness when they had done wrong.

Then the Lord said, "Remember, I am the Lord who brought you out of Egypt. Be holy, for I am holy."

Then the Lord asked the Israelites to set aside a special day to celebrate their deliverance from the Egyptians. It was called the Passover. They were to remember the Lord's deliverance when the death angel had "passed over" every Israelite home that had the lamb's blood smeared on the doorposts. They were learning that God is holy, good, wise, and faithful.

Affirmation: I will be holy!

Whisper A Prayer In The Morning

Be holy, for I am holy. (Leviticus 11:45)

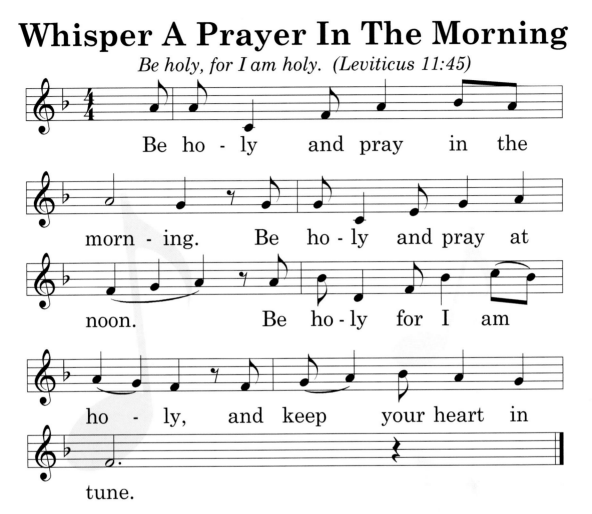

Be ho - ly and pray in the morn - ing. Be ho - ly and pray at noon. Be ho - ly for I am ho - ly, and keep your heart in tune.

God answers prayer in the morning. God answers prayer at noon. God answers prayer in the evening. So keep your heart in tune.

UMBERS

DONKEY TALK *Numbers 22*

The Israelites traveled on to the plain of Moab and camped near the Jordan River. The Moabites were frightened to see so many people. "What if they attack us?" they said. "We will be destroyed!" So the king of Moab sent messengers to find the prophet named Balaam. They asked Balaam to put a curse on the Israelites so the Moabites could defeat them in battle.

Balaam said, "Spend the night here. I will ask God what He wants me to do." That night, the Lord spoke to Balaam, "Do not go with these men. You must never curse My people who are blessed." When he told the messengers that the Lord would not allow him to curse the Israelites, they said, "Don't let God stop you from doing this. We will pay you lots of money." Balaam was tempted by what they were offering and said, "I'll ask God again."

The next day Balaam got up, saddled his donkey, and left with the messengers of Moab. God was very angry that Balaam had disobeyed. He sent an angel with a drawn sword to stand in the road to block the way. Balaam's donkey saw the angel and turned off the road into a field. Balaam beat his donkey for doing this. But he could not see the angel. This happened a second and third time until finally the Lord opened the donkey's mouth and she said to Balaam, "What have I done to you to make you beat me three times?"

Balaam couldn't believe his ears! "A talking donkey?" he thought. "You are acting crazy. If I had a sword I'd kill you right here!" Then the Lord opened Balaam's eyes and he saw the angel of the Lord standing in the road with his sword drawn. "Your donkey saw me and turned away from me three times. If she had not, I would have killed you, for you have disobeyed the Lord, and I am sent to stop you."

Balaam said to the angel, "I have sinned. I will turn around and go back." The angel said, "Go on with these men, but speak only what I tell you." Balaam agreed and went on with the messengers to meet with the king of Moab. Instead of cursing the God of Israel, he praised the Lord again and again for His goodness and faithfulness.

The king was furious. "Go! I told you to curse my enemies, not bless them." Then the prophet Balaam told the king that Moab would soon be defeated, and out of Israel would come a great ruler. The king went away very sad.

Affirmation: I will praise the Lord for His goodness!

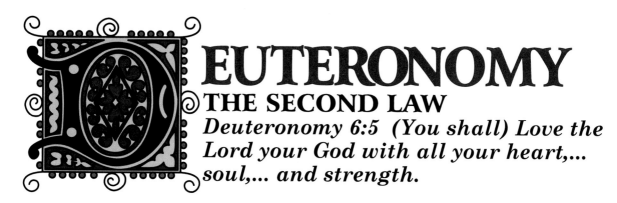

DEUTERONOMY
THE SECOND LAW
Deuteronomy 6:5 (You shall) Love the Lord your God with all your heart,... soul,... and strength.

Moses continued to teach the word of the Lord to the children of Israel. He spoke these beautiful words: "Hear, O Israel. The Lord our God, the Lord is one. You shall love the Lord your God with all your heart, soul, and strength."

"Think about His commandments every day. Teach them to your children. Talk about them when you are sitting at home or away from home. Even before you close your eyes at night, remember God's goodness."

"Fear the Lord and serve Him only. Do not be persuaded by your friends to disobey the Lord, for this is not pleasing to the Lord. Keep His commandments and love Him always." Moses taught the people of Israel how to live a godly life.

After many years of traveling and learning about God, the children of Israel were now ready to enter the land God had promised them. Joshua was appointed to lead the people into the promised land.

As the people prepared to cross the Jordan River into the promised land, Moses spoke to them one last time. "Remember the greatness of our God. Obey His commands and you will be a great nation." Then he sang a praise hymn to the Lord.

Moses climbed up the high mountain called Nebo, and the Lord showed Moses the land promised to Abraham, Isaac, and Jacob. He could see the city of Jericho all the way to the sea.

After Moses had seen this, he died and was received into heaven. The people of Israel were very sad Moses had died for he was a great man of God.

Affirmation: I am thankful for God's goodness!

I've Got The Joy, Joy, Joy, Joy Down In My Heart

You shall love the Lord your God with all your heart, soul, and strength. (Deuteronomy 6:5)

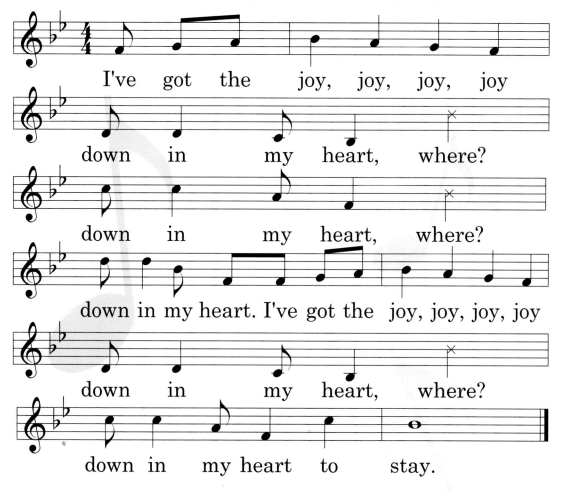

I've got the joy, joy, joy, joy

down in my heart, where?

down in my heart, where?

down in my heart. I've got the joy, joy, joy, joy

down in my heart, where?

down in my heart to stay.

Verse II: I've got the wonderful love of my blessed Redeemer way down in the depths of my heart to stay.

Verse III: You shall love the Lord, your God, with all your heart and soul and strength always.

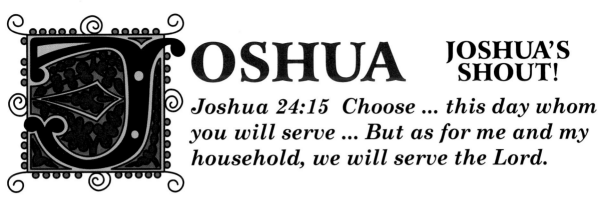

JOSHUA

JOSHUA'S SHOUT!

Joshua 24:15 Choose ... this day whom you will serve ... But as for me and my household, we will serve the Lord.

After Moses died, the Lord spoke to Joshua saying, "Get ready to cross the Jordan River. The promised land awaits you. I will walk with you, Joshua, as I did with Moses. I will make you a strong leader, so be courageous and obey My laws."

Joshua shouted to the people, "Get ready, for in three days we cross the Jordan River into the promised land!"

At that time there were people already living in Canaan. Joshua knew that he must defeat them if they were going to possess the land. Wisely, he sent two spies into the great walled city of Jericho. Soon, he would know their strength and if they were preparing for battle.

The two spies secretly crossed the Jordan and entered Jericho. They stayed with a woman named Rahab, but the king soon found out!

He sent messengers to Rahab who said, "Bring out the two men who are spying on us. We know they're here!" Secretly, Rahab had hidden the two men on the roof of her house. "They were here, but they're gone. Perhaps you can catch them on the road if you hurry."

Just before nightfall, Rahab went back to the roof and said to the spies, "I have helped you, now you must help me. I know that the Lord is mighty and He has given this land to you."

"When the battle comes, save me and my family."
The men agreed that if Rahab would not tell the king
about them, they would save her family. Rahab's
house was part of the great wall, so that night the
men climbed out of Rahab's window, down a long
rope and escaped into the hills. The spies returned
to Joshua, "The Lord is surely giving our people this
land. The Canaanites are afraid of us!"

Three days later, Joshua said to the people,
"Tomorrow we cross the Jordan River. The ark of the
Lord will go before you. Follow behind it, for great is
our Lord!" Then came another miracle. As soon as
the priests carrying the ark set foot in the rushing
current of the Jordan River, the waters stopped
flowing. The Israelites could then pass through the
river on dry ground. God had made a way like He
had done at the Red Sea! Not until the last person
came out of the river did the waters flow again.

As Joshua neared the city of Jericho, he met a
strange man with his sword drawn. Joshua went to
him and said, "Are you for us or against us?"

"I command the invisible army of the Lord," he
replied. Joshua fell face down with fear and respect.
Then the Lord told Joshua what he must do to win
the coming battle.

The day of the battle came. Seven priests blowing seven trumpets marched around the city of Jericho one time. The ark of the Lord was right behind them. An armed guard marched ahead of the priests and followed up behind the ark. They circled Jericho once and no one spoke a single word. "What are they doing?" cried the people of Jericho. "God is going to destroy us!"
They were afraid.

God commanded Joshua and his army to march around the city each day for six days. On the seventh day, the people marched around Jericho seven times. But the seventh time, just as the priests sounded the trumpet blast, Joshua commanded the nation, "Shout! For the Lord has given you the city! Shout! Shout!"

The people shouted
and the trumpets blasted, louder
and louder, until the walls of Jericho began to crack
and came tumbling down! The city was captured. Rahab
and her family who had helped them were saved.

Affirmation: The Lord is mighty!

Joshua Fit the Battle of Jericho

Joshua 24:15 Choose ... this day whom you will serve ... But as for me and my household, we will serve the Lord.

 **UDGES** **MIGHTY SAMSON**

Judges 16:28 O Lord (my) God, please remember me and strengthen me.

When Joshua was 110 years old, he died. Joshua's life had pleased the Lord. But the children and grandchildren of the Israelites were doing things that did not please the Lord.

On a day when Israel had fallen into sin, the Lord allowed the Philistines to make them slaves.

At the very same time the angel of the Lord appeared to an Israelite woman who was unable to have children and said, "You will soon have a little baby boy.

Therefore, do not drink any wine while you are pregnant.

When the baby is born, do not cut his hair, for he has been chosen to serve the Lord and deliver Israel from the Philistines."

A little baby boy named Samson was born. He grew to be very strong, and the Lord blessed him.

139

When Samson became a man, he fell in love with a woman named Delilah. She did not believe in God. The Philistine rulers went to her and said, "Find out what makes Samson so strong and we will give you lots of money." She agreed.

Delilah begged Samson to tell her the secret of his strength, but he would not. Three times she asked, but Samson would not tell her. Finally, he said, "My hair has never been cut, because I was set apart to God since birth. If my head were shaved, I would become as weak as any other man."

So Delilah went straight to the rulers and told them the secret of Samson's strength. That night while Samson slept, she let the Philistines in to shave his head. With his strength gone, Samson was blinded and put into prison. The people celebrated and shouted, "Bring out Samson that he may amuse us!"

They set Samson between the two support pillars of the temple. Now the temple was very crowded that day. Three thousand men and women were on the roof watching. Then Samson prayed, "O Lord my

God, please remember me and strengthen me." Samson gave a mighty push on the pillars. They began to crack into pieces and suddenly, the whole temple fell killing Samson and all the people in it.

Affirmation: The Lord is my strength!

Do Lord, Remember Me

O Lord (my) God, please remember
me and strengthen me. (Judges 16:28)

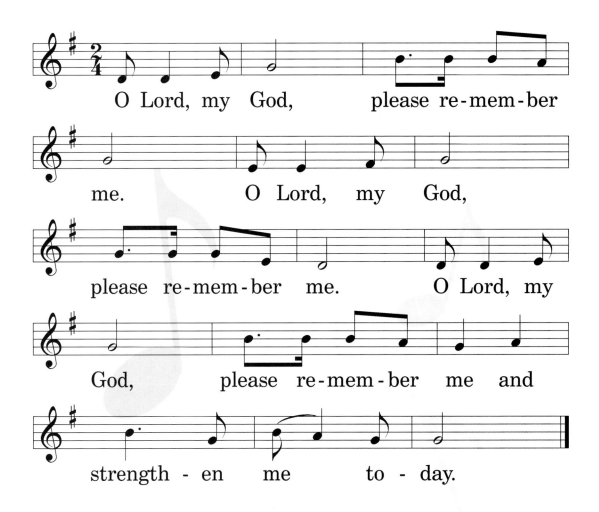

O Lord, my God, please re-mem-ber
me. O Lord, my God,
please re-mem-ber me. O Lord, my
God, please re-mem-ber me and
strength - en me to - day.

Verse II: Samson was a mighty man, a mighty man was he. Samson was a mighty man, a mighty man was he. Samson was a mighty man, a mighty man was he. Samson feared the Lord.

RUTH

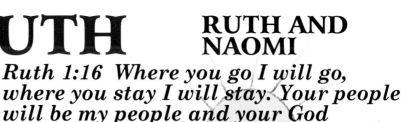

Ruth 1:16 Where you go I will go, where you stay I will stay. Your people will be my people and your God my God.

The judges were ruling Israel in the days when a terrible famine came. A man named Elimelech, his wife Naomi, and their two sons left Bethlehem and moved to Moab where there was plenty of food. While in Moab, Elimelech died, leaving Naomi alone with two sons. Sometime later, her sons married Moabite women named Orpah and Ruth.

143

They lived as a happy family for about ten years, and then both of her sons died. When Naomi learned that the famine in Judah had ended, she prepared to leave Moab and return home. Ruth and Orpah walked with Naomi part of the way because they loved her very much. Naomi said, "Each of you must go back to your mother's house. May the Lord show kindness to you."

Orpah returned home to her mother, but Ruth said, "Where you go I will go. Your people will be my people, and your God my God."

So the two women traveled on to Bethlehem where the barley harvest had just begun. It was a custom in those days that the poor would follow behind the harvesters and pick up any barley left behind. It was called "gleaning."

"I will go to the fields and glean," Ruth told Naomi. Ruth began working in a field owned by a man named Boaz, a relative of Naomi's.

Boaz noticed how hard Ruth was working and asked who she was. "She's a young woman from Moab who returned with Naomi," answered the foreman. Boaz liked Ruth and said, "Please stay close by and do not glean anywhere else. Stay near the other women and I'll make sure you are protected."

Ruth bowed and said, "Why are you being so kind to me?" Boaz replied, "I've heard how you left your home to care for Naomi. May the Lord bless you for what you have done."

Boaz helped Ruth in many ways. He made sure that she had enough to eat. He admired her very much because she always took care of Naomi. Boaz fell in love with Ruth and asked her to marry him. They were married one sunny day and soon a baby named Obed was born. He would be the father of Jesse who would be the father of David, the king of Israel. Naomi continued to live with Ruth and Boaz, and was very happy.

Affirmation: I will be a friend to others!

Na-Naomi

Where you go I will go, where you stay I will stay. Your people
will be my people and your God my God. (Ruth 1:16)

Na, na, na, na, na, na, na, na, na, na, Na, na, na,

na, na, na, na, na, na, na, Na, Na-o-mi,

Na, na, na, Na-o-mi where are you go-ing this

won-der-ful day? Na, Na-o-mi,

Na, na, na, Na-o-mi where are you go-ing this

won-der-ful day? Where you go, I will go.

Where you stay I will stay. Your peo-ple will

be my peo-ple. Your God will be my God.

First
SAMUEL
DAVID AND GOLIATH

1 Samuel 16:7 For man looks at the outward appearance, but (God) the Lord looks at the heart.

Samuel was the last judge to rule Israel. The people of Israel decided they wanted a king, so Samuel chose Saul.

Saul became the first king of Israel.

Israel met the Philistine army on the battlefield. The Israelites made camp on one hill and the Philistines camped on another with a wide valley between them. Now the Philistines had a champion warrior named Goliath. Goliath stood over nine feet tall and carried a heavy javelin and sword. His armor was made of bronze and glistened in the sunlight.

Each morning for forty days the giant Goliath came forward and shouted like thunder, "We don't need to have a war today. Send out one man to fight me. If your man defeats me, all the Philistines will be your slaves. But if I win you will serve us!" King Saul and all the Israelites were terrified. Who could defeat such a giant?

One morning, Jesse, son of Obed, sent his youngest son David to the battlefield to deliver a meal to David's older brothers who were soldiers.

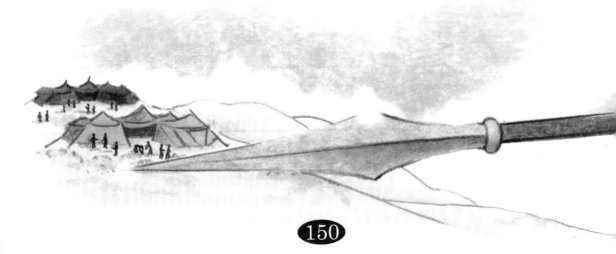

150

When David arrived and heard Goliath mocking the Lord's army, he said to Saul, "Do not fear this Philistine. I will go and fight him!"

"You? Fight the giant? Why, you are only a boy," scoffed Saul. "He is a mighty warrior, a killer. You are a shepherd boy. You cannot fight him." Then David answered, "As I kept my father's sheep, I once fought a lion and rescued the sheep. When the lion turned on me, I killed it. Later, when a bear came to take away the sheep, I killed the bear. This giant will be defeated just like them, for the Lord who delivered me from the lion and the bear will deliver me from the hand of this Philistine." Saul said, "Go, and the Lord be with you!"

David put on Saul's armor, but he was not used to it. "I cannot wear this armor," David said. So he gathered his staff, five stones, and his slingshot and started walking directly toward Goliath.

When Goliath saw that Israel had sent a young boy to fight him, he grew angry. "Am I a dog that you come at me with a stick? Come here and I'll tear you apart!" Then David spoke, "You come against me with a sword and a spear, but I come against you in the name of the Lord Almighty, the God of Israel's army, whom you mock. This day you will die!"

Goliath was furious and moved in to attack.
But David took out one of the stones
and loaded it into his slingshot.
With all the power of the Lord behind
him, he let it go. Bam! It struck
Goliath right in the forehead
and sank deep.

Goliath staggered, his knees buckled, and he fell like a giant oak tree. Goliath was not dead, so David ran and stood over Goliath. Taking Goliath's own sword, he killed him.

The Lord had given Israel the battle. The Philistine army ran away, but Israel went after them and defeated them. From that day on, David remained in King Saul's service.

Affirmation:
I will stand up
for the Lord!

Only A Boy Named David

For man looks at the outward appearance,
but (God) the Lord looks at the heart. (1 Samuel 16:7)

On-ly a boy named Da-vid, on-ly a lit-tle sling,

on-ly a boy named Da-vid, but he could pray and sing.

On-ly a boy named Da-vid, on-ly a rip-p'ling brook,

on-ly a boy named Da-vid, but five lit-tle stones he took. And

one lit-tle stone went in-to the sling and laugh-ter did im-part. For

man looks on the out-ward, but God looks on the heart. And

round and round and round and round and

round and round and round, then one lit-tle stone went up in the air

and the gi-ant came tum-ba-ling down.

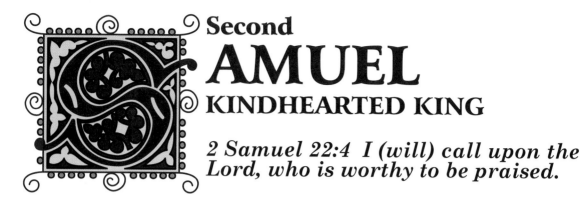

Second SAMUEL
KINDHEARTED KING

2 Samuel 22:4 I (will) call upon the Lord, who is worthy to be praised.

During a fierce battle with the Philistine army, King Saul found his army outnumbered and fled. Saul and his three sons, including Jonathan, were all killed that day. David became the new king of Israel.

David did not know that Jonathan, his dearest friend, had a five-year-old son named Mephibosheth. In that day when a new king came to the throne, he would search for the children of the old king and have them sent away or killed so they could never be king. That is why Mephibosheth's nurse took the boy and fled for safety. In her haste, she stumbled and dropped the little boy, crippling him for life.

One day, King David asked if any of Saul's family was alive. He wanted to show them kindness because of his promise to Jonathan. A former servant to Saul named Ziba told him Jonathan's crippled son Mephibosheth was indeed alive. David sent for him and he was brought to the palace. Mephibosheth must have thought David was going to kill him. He fell on his face and cried, "Here is your servant."

But David said, "Don't be afraid. I will give back to you all the land your grandfather Saul owned and you shall always be welcome at my dinner table." Because of David's kindness, Mephibosheth became a part of the king's family.

Affirmation: I will show kindness to others!

I Will Call Upon The Lord

I (will) call upon the Lord, who is worthy to be praised.
(2 Samuel 22:4)

I will call up - on the Lord

who is wor - thy to be praised.

I will call up - on the Lord, I will

call up - on the Lord to - day.

I will call up - on the Lord

who is wor - thy to be praised.

I will call up - on the Lord, I will

call up - on the Lord to - day.

First
KINGS
AHAB AND JEZEBEL'S FIREFALL
1 Kings 16-18

Some years after Solomon died, Ahab became king of Israel. He was the most wicked king to ever reign over Israel. He and his evil wife Jezebel led the Israelites in the worship of Baal, a false god. Now there appeared before Ahab a prophet named Elijah. Elijah told Ahab, "Because of your great wickedness, it will not rain unless I say so."

Then the Lord sent Elijah eastward to hide. There he drank from a crystal clear brook, and the Lord ordered ravens to bring him bread and meat.

Elijah stayed hidden for three years, and just as he said it did not rain during this time. Then the Lord told Elijah to return to Ahab and he would send rain. When Ahab saw Elijah he said, "Is it really you, the big trouble-maker of Israel?" Elijah said, "Not I, but you and your family have caused Israel's trouble by worshiping Baal. Call for your priests and meet me on Mount Carmel."

When they were all gathered on the mountain, Elijah spoke. "Will you ever make up your mind? If the Lord Yahweh is God, follow him; but if Baal is God, follow him. I am the only prophet of Yahweh here today. There are 450 prophets of Baal here. Therefore, I challenge you.

Prepare two bulls for sacrifice and lay them on a bed of wood. All of you call on your god and I alone will call on mine. The one who answers with fire from heaven is the true god." They agreed to his challenge.

All day long the priests of Baal called on their false god, but nothing happened. Elijah laughed at them, "Shout louder, maybe he's gone on vacation." Finally, Elijah called to the people, "Come to me." They watched as Elijah built an altar with twelve stones. Then he had them pour twelve barrels of water on his firewood. Elijah called to the Lord, "Today, O Lord, let it be known that You are the one true God."

Instantly fire fell from heaven burning up the meat, the wood, even the stones. "Kill these false prophets," demanded Elijah. And it was done. Soon the skies darkened and the rain began to fall. Elijah's God was the one true God.

Affirmation: I will praise the Lord of heaven, the one true God.

Second KINGS

ELIJAH AND THE CHARIOT OF FIRE

2 Kings 18:22 We trust in the Lord our God.

Elijah and Elisha were traveling from city to city proclaiming the name of the Lord when God decided to take Elijah up to heaven. It seemed that everywhere they went, other prophets knew Elijah's earthly ministry was about to end. But Elisha asked them not to speak about it. Finally, Elijah, Elisha, and about 50 followers reached the banks of the Jordan River.

Elijah took off his coat, rolled it up, and struck the water with it. The waters of the Jordan parted to the left and right making a pathway to cross through. Only Elijah and Elisha walked across the river. "Can I give you any blessing before I leave you?" Elijah asked Elisha. Elisha answered, "Let me have your faith and love in a double measure."

Elijah sighed, "What you ask is very hard to do, but if you see me when I leave this earth, it will be yours."

As they were walking and talking together, suddenly a chariot of fire pulled by horses of fire appeared from the sky and drove between the two men. In an instant, Elijah went up into heaven in a whirlwind.

Elisha saw this and shouted, "My Father! My Father! The chariots and horsemen of Israel!" Then Elijah and the chariot were gone.

Elisha humbled himself before the Lord by tearing his clothes. He picked up Elijah's coat which had fallen and dipped it into the Jordan River. The waters parted again and Elisha crossed to join the other followers. They all bowed before Elisha, for they knew the Spirit of God was with him.

Affirmation: I will seek the Spirit of God!

Praise Ye, The Lord

We trust in the Lord our God. (2 Kings 18:22)

E - li-jah went up in a char-i-ot of fi-re,

Praise ye, the Lord. E - li-jah went up in a

char-i-ot of fi-re, Praise ye, the Lord.

Praise ye the Lord, Hal-le-lu-jah! Praise ye the

Lord, Hal-le-lu-jah! Praise ye the

Lord, Hal-le-lu-jah! Praise ye the Lord!

Verse II: We trust in the Lord, our God and King. Praise ye the Lord. We trust in the Lord, our God and King. Praise ye the Lord. Praise ye the Lord, hallelujah. Praise ye the Lord, hallelujah. Praise ye the Lord, hallelujah. Praise ye the Lord.

First
CHRONICLES
THE ARK OF THE COVENANT

1 Chronicles 16:8 O give thanks unto the Lord, call upon his name.

Before King David died, he had the ark of the Lord brought to Jerusalem. The ark, a reminder of God's power and presence, was the same ark that traveled with Moses and Joshua. It was a large chest which was kept in the most holy place of the Lord's temple. Inside the chest they kept three things: the tablets of the Ten Commandments, the pot of manna, and Aaron's rod which had budded in the wilderness with Moses.

Now David directed the priests to preach and praise the Lord while standing before the ark. They were to play musical instruments like the harp, the cymbals, and the trumpets as they worshiped. David wrote a psalm which was sung in that day:

O give thanks unto the Lord,

Call upon His name.

O sing to Him, sing praise to Him

And tell of His mighty deeds.

Glory in His holy name.

Let those who seek the Lord rejoice.

Affirmation: I will give thanks unto the Lord!

Second
CHRONICLES
JOSIAH: A TEENAGER FINDS A TREASURE

2 Chronicles 7:14 If my people, who are called by my name, will humble themselves and pray ... I will hear from heaven and will forgive their sin and will heal their land.

When Josiah was eight years old, his father King Amon died making Josiah king. King Amon had disobeyed the Lord, as did his father King Manasseh. They worshiped idols, but Josiah loved the Lord God and sought to please him in every way. So, while he was still very young, he destroyed the idols that were in Judah. Then he sent workers to repair the temple of the Lord.

While the workers were cleaning the temple, they found Israel's treasure. There in the dust was the Book of the Law written by Moses. It had been lost for many years. Shaphan, the scribe, took the scroll and ran to the palace. There he read the law to young King Josiah. The law warned Israel that if they disobeyed the commandments, God would send great trouble upon them. Josiah asked God for forgiveness for the way his people had sinned. He called all the people of Israel together and read the law and promised to obey it.

Affirmation: I will read my Bible each day!

I Will Hear From Heaven

If my people, who are called by my name, will humble themselves and pray ... I will hear from heaven and will forgive their sin and will heal their land. (2 Chronicles 7:14)

If my peo-ple who are called by my name will hum-ble them-selves and pray, If my peo-ple who are called by my name will hum-ble them-selves and pray, I will hear from hea-ven and for - give their sins, hear from hea-ven and I'll heal their land. If my peo-ple who are called by my name will hum - ble them-selves and pray.

Verse I: When trouble comes a-calling, asking for you, humble yourselves and pray. When trouble comes a-calling, here's what to do, humble yourselves and pray.

Verse II: When sickness comes a-calling, asking for you, humble yourselves and pray. When sickness comes a-calling, here's what to do. Humble yourselves and pray.

EZRA

MIXED-UP BUILDERS

Ezra 3:11 With praise and thanksgiving they sang to the Lord: He is good; his love to Israel endures forever.

The prophet Ezra tells the story of the Israelites' return from Babylon. Now free from slavery, King Cyrus ordered the temple to be rebuilt.

Ezra also had the king's blessing to choose judges and rulers who knew the laws of God. Ezra was to teach Israel how to live God's way. "Praise be to the Lord," said Ezra, "for a king who honors the Lord."

This made the Jews very happy. Everyone brought gold and silver and precious oils and ointments to be used in rebuilding the temple.

People who were already living in the land also came to help. These people worshiped the God of heaven and false gods at the same time. This displeased the Lord. So the Jews decided to rebuild the temple without the help of people who dishonored the Lord.

This made the people very angry, so they tried to stop the building. When King Cyrus died, armed men forced the work to stop. But God sent two prophets, Haggai and Zechariah, to encourage the people to start building again. "We can do it without the help of idol worshipers. Arise and build!" When the new king, Darius, blessed the Jews and allowed them to rebuild, it was an answer to prayer.

Affirmation: I will be faithful to serve the Lord!

With Praise and Thanksgiving

With praise and thanksgiving they sang to the Lord:
He is good; his love to Israel endures forever. (Ezra 3:11)

With praise and thanks-giv-ing they sang un-to the Lord. With praise and thanks-giv-ing they sang un-to the Lord. Our God, He is good. Our God, He is good. His love to Is-ra-el en-dures. Our God, He is good.

Verse II: Yes, we are the servants of the God of heaven and earth. Yes, we are the servants of the God of heaven and earth. Our God, He is good. Our God, He is good. His love to Israel endures. Our God, He is good.

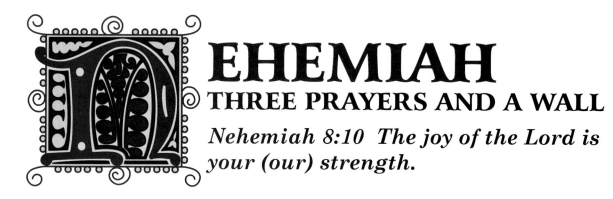

NEHEMIAH
THREE PRAYERS AND A WALL

Nehemiah 8:10 The joy of the Lord is your (our) strength.

There once lived an Israelite named Nehemiah who was a servant of the Persian king Artaxerxes. One day, he learned that the great wall of Jerusalem was broken down and needed repair. Without a wall of defense, Jerusalem might be attacked by enemies. Nehemiah wept and did not eat food. He knew that prayer could change everything.

"O Lord," he prayed, "we have not obeyed your commands; please forgive us and grant that the king will allow me to return to Jerusalem to rebuild the wall."

The next time Nehemiah waited upon the king, Artaxerxes asked, "Why are you so sad, Nehemiah?" He answered, "I have heard that Jerusalem lies in ruin, the walls are falling down, and the gates destroyed by fire!"

Then the king said, "What can I do to help you?" Nehemiah prayed again before he answered. He said, "Send me, O King, to rebuild the walls!" God answered Nehemiah's prayers and the king granted his request to go to Jerusalem.

Nehemiah traveled 700 miles to Jerusalem. No one but the king knew of Nehemiah's plans. When he arrived, he looked at the broken down walls and gates in the darkness of night. When Nehemiah figured out how big the job was and how long it would take, he said, "Come let us rebuild the walls. We will no longer be ashamed and the king has blessed us!"

The people cheered, "Let us rebuild!" So they began the work. But mockers came and tried to discourage them. For the third time, Nehemiah prayed, "The God of heaven, He will give us success. Therefore, we His servants will arise and build!" Prayer can really change things! Over the next 52 days the wall was rebuilt. It was an answer to Nehemiah's prayer.

Affirmation: I will pray each day!

Building For The Lord

The joy of the Lord is your (our) strength. (Nehemiah 8:10)

Build - ing, build - ing, build - ing for the Lord,

Build - ing, build - ing, build - ing for the Lord, with a

kind word or com - pli - ment, a friend - ly how - dy - do, Will

lead them to the Sav - ior, That's

what we all should do. The

joy of the Lord is our strength to - day. The

joy of the Lord is mine. It keeps me strong when

things go wrong, the joy of the Lord is our strength.

179

ESTHER

BRAVE AND BEAUTIFUL QUEEN

Esther 4:14 And who knows but that you have come to royal position for such a time as this?

Once, in the city of Susa the capital of Persia, great king Xerxes gave a banquet in honor of his many governors. As the banquet went on, King Xerxes called for Vashti the queen. "Place the royal crown on Vashti's head and bring her to me," commanded the king, for she was very beautiful.

When Queen Vashti refused to come, the king was very angry. He sent Vashti away and ordered a nationwide search for a new queen.

Now there was a Jewish man named Mordecai who also lived in Persia. He had a beautiful cousin named Esther. In obedience to the king's order, Esther was taken to the king's palace. Mordecai asked her to tell no one that she was Jewish.

When the king saw Esther, he loved her. He set the royal crown on her head and made her the new queen.

One day Mordecai was sitting at the king's gate waiting to see Esther. He heard two soldiers planning to kill the king. Mordecai told Esther, who in turn, told the king. "Mordecai has told me of a plot to kill you, my King!" said Esther. The king had the two men arrested and they were found guilty. Mordecai had saved the king's life and it was written down in the history books.

After this, King Xerxes honored Haman by making him second in command of Persia. Haman was a very proud man and at the king's order everyone was to bow before him. But Mordecai would bow to no one except the Lord. This angered Haman. When he later found out that Mordecai was an Israelite, he began to look for a way to destroy them all. Then he came up with an evil plan.

Haman went to King Xerxes and said, "There are people in your kingdom who do not obey your laws, O King, but rather God's laws. This is not good for us. Therefore, let us send soldiers to kill them." The king agreed, so Haman sent out an order to kill the Jews.

When Mordecai heard about Haman's evil plan, he sent word to Esther. "Perhaps God has made you Queen of Persia for such a time as this. Maybe He will use you to save His people."

Then Esther sent word back to Mordecai. "Gather all the Jews in Susa and pray for three days. Though it is against the law for me to go to the king, I will do so. Pray that the king will have mercy and stop Haman's evil plan." Mordecai did as Esther asked.

On the third day, Esther prepared a banquet and only invited the king and Haman. "What can I do for you?" the king asked. "Name it and it will be done." Esther spoke, "Will you and Haman come tomorrow to another special banquet? Then I will tell you both."

As Haman left,
he again passed Mordecai at the
gate. Again, Mordecai refused to bow. Haman in
his anger decided to start building the place where
Mordecai would be executed. That night, as the king
was reading the history book, he discovered he had not
honored Mordecai for saving his life. He called Haman
and said, "I want to honor a special man. What should I do?"

Haman thought he was the man to be honored, so he said,
"Let him wear the royal robe and be put on the king's horse
and lead him through the city proclaiming, "The king is
honoring this man!" So Haman was asked to honor
Mordecai in this way. Haman was furious.

Later, Haman and the king went to dine with Esther. "What is your request? Tell me and it shall be yours," said the king to Esther. "O King, spare me and the life of my people."

"Spare you? You are queen!" said the king. "Yes," said Esther, "but I am also a Jew. And there is a man in the kingdom who wants to kill all of the jews."

"Who is this man?" asked the king. "Haman," she replied. "He is an evil man."

The king was furious and that night Haman was hanged on the very gallows he had built for Mordecai. God's people were saved!

Affirmation: I will kneel and pray to God alone!

For Such A Time As This

And who knows but that you have come to royal
position for such a time as this? *(Esther 4:14)*

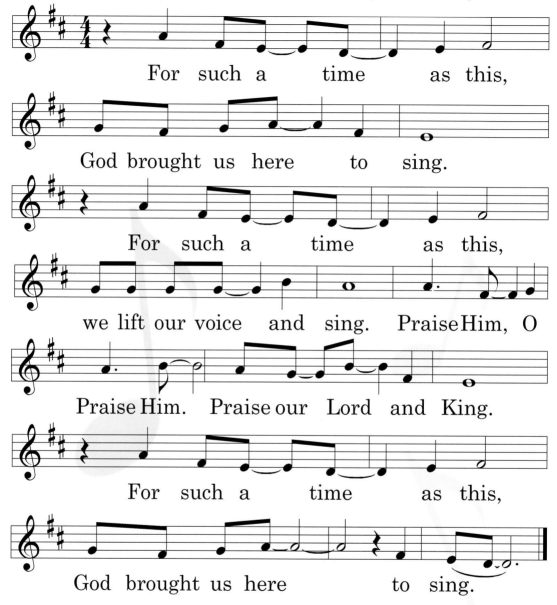

For such a time as this,

God brought us here to sing.

For such a time as this,

we lift our voice and sing. Praise Him, O

Praise Him. Praise our Lord and King.

For such a time as this,

God brought us here to sing.

Bridge: And who knows but that you've come here for such a time as
this. Who knows, maybe we can change our world.

JOB

JOB'S TROUBLE

Job 19:25 I know that my Redeemer lives, and that in the end he will stand upon the earth.

Once, in the land of Uz there lived a man named Job. Job and his wife had seven wonderful sons and three beautiful daughters. Job was a good man in the eyes of the Lord and his life was a blessing to others.

Job was also very wealthy. He owned 7,000 sheep, 3,000 camels, 500 oxen, and 500 donkeys, and had many servants. Early in the morning Job would kneel and pray and thank God for his family. He loved them very much.

Now one day in the kingdom of heaven, the angels were coming before the Lord to praise Him. Suddenly, Satan made an appearance. "Where have you come from?" the Lord asked Satan. "I've been roaming the earth, tempting your people to do evil," shouted Satan. "Then you have seen My servant Job," the Lord said. "He hates evil and is always faithful to serve Me." Satan responded, "He only loves You because You protect his family and You've made him very rich. Take that away and he'll hate you!"

"Very well," said the Lord, "I give you permission to test Job. But do no harm to the man."

A few days later a messenger came running to Job and said, "The Sabeans have stolen your oxen and donkeys and killed your servants! I alone have escaped." He had not finished speaking when in came a second servant. "Fire has fallen from out of the sky and burned up all your sheep and your servants! I alone have escaped to tell you." And while he was still speaking, in came a third messenger, "The Chaldeans have attacked us and stolen your camels! They have killed all the servants, and I alone have escaped to tell you."

And before he could finish speaking, in came a fourth servant who said, "Your sons and daughters were together eating dinner when suddenly a strong wind came from the desert and blew down the house, killing them all!"

Job stood before them and sorrow overcame him. His children, his servants, and his possessions were gone! He tore his robe and fell to the ground with a broken heart. He prayed, "I came into this world with nothing. Surely I will leave with nothing. It is the Lord who gives; it is the Lord who has taken away. Praise the name of the Lord!" Job did not blame God for his trouble. This pleased the Lord.

Once again, Satan appeared before the God of Heaven. The Lord spoke, "Your evil schemes have not worked, have they? Job is still faithful to Me!" Then Satan lashed out, "Yes, but if You allow me to cause him great sickness and pain, he will curse You!"

"Very well," said the Lord, "do as you wish, but do not kill Job." So Satan caused Job's skin to be covered with painful sores from head to toe. Job's heart was breaking for his children, and his body was terribly sick. Job's wife said, "Why should you be faithful to the Lord now? Look at you! Look at our family! You should curse God and die!" But Job replied, "Shall we accept the good and not the trouble?" And again, Job did not blame God.

Job had three close friends who came to comfort him. They hardly recognized their friend because of his sickness and grief. They sat with Job for seven days and nights without saying a word. Finally, Job spoke and cursed the day he was born.

His friend Eliphaz spoke first, "The Lord is correcting you for an evil you have done."

"What kind of friends are you to tell me I have done wrong when I have not?" cried Job.

Then his friend Bildad spoke, "Somewhere, you have forgotten the Lord. So pray that He might forgive you and take away this sickness and pain." Job spoke up, "I have not sinned and all I want to know is why God has done this to me."

Then the Lord spoke to Job out of a storm. "Now I will ask the questions and you will answer. Where were you when I created the world, when I gave orders to the morning? Where were you when I created the seas and formed a man? Can you speak to the clouds and give strength to all creatures? Does the hawk fly by your wisdom; does the eagle soar at your command? Now, do you stand and accuse God Almighty of evil? Answer Me!"

Then Job understood. There are things which we cannot understand, things that only God can know, and we must not question. For men and women are not equal to God. Job bowed his head and prayed, "I am nothing, Lord. Forgive me."

The Lord was pleased with Job and asked him to forgive his friends, for they, too, did not understand the power and greatness of God. After Job had prayed for his friends, the Lord gave Job twice as much as he had before and Job's life was blessed.

Affirmation: I will not blame God for my troubles!

I Know That My Redeemer Lives

I know that my Redeemer lives, and that in the end he will stand upon the earth. (Job 19:25)

I know that my Re - deem - er lives.

What com-fort this sweet sen - tence gives.

And in the end He will stand up-on the earth. The

dead in Christ shall rise, O glor-ious birth.

I know that my Re - deem - er lives.

And all trans-gress - ions He for-gives.

Though death shall come I will trust my soul to Thee.

Safe in the hands of God e - ter-nal-ly.

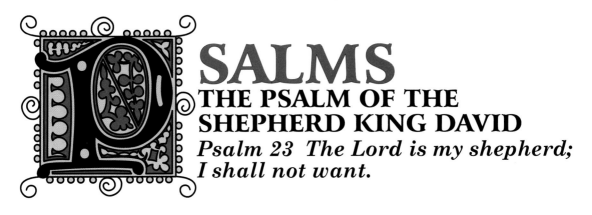

PSALMS
THE PSALM OF THE SHEPHERD KING DAVID
Psalm 23 The Lord is my shepherd;
I shall not want.

The Lord is my shepherd, I shall not want.
He makes me to lie down in green pastures.
He leads me beside the still waters.
He restores my soul.
He leads me in the paths of righteousness
*   for His name's sake.*
Yea though I walk through the valley of the shadow of death,
I will fear no evil, for You are with me.
Your rod and Your staff, they comfort me.
You prepare a table before me
*   in the presence of my enemies.*
You anoint my head with oil.
My cup runs over.
Surely goodness and mercy shall follow me
*   all the days of my life,*
And I will dwell in the house of the Lord
Forever.

Affirmation: I will trust the Lord, my shepherd!

The Lord Is My Shepherd

The Lord is my shepherd; I shall not want. (Psalm 23:1)

The   Lord   is   my shep-herd,   the

Lord is my shep-herd, the Lord is my shep-herd and I

shall not want. The   Lord is my shep-herd, the

Lord   is   my   shep - herd,   the

Lord is my shep - herd and I   shall not want. He

makes   me   lie down   in green   past - ures.   He

leads me be-side still   wa - ters.   He re-stores my

soul   and   guides me where   I   go.   The

PROVERBS
CHILDREN OF WISDOM

Proverbs 3:5 Trust in the Lord with all your heart.

King Solomon, the son of David, wrote the book of Proverbs to help us live godly lives in an ungodly world. "Wisdom" is the key word in this book. "Having wisdom" means that we live our lives as God would have us live. Wisdom will keep us from making mistakes. Here are some key verses of wisdom from the book of Proverbs:

Trust in the Lord with all your heart and lean not upon your own understanding; in all your ways acknowledge Him and He will direct your path.

The fear and respect of the Lord is the beginning of wisdom.

Respect and fear the Lord and stop doing evil things. This will cause you to be healthier and happier.

If the Lord loves you, He may test you. Do not be angry at the Lord if this happens.

A wise son makes his father glad, but an unwise son causes his mother to be grieved.

Even a child is known by what he does.

Train up a child in the ways of the Lord and when he grows older, he will not depart from them.

Do not withhold correction from a child, for if you discipline him, he will not die.

Be honest with everyone. Tell the truth and do not lie.

Affirmation: I will love and obey my parents!

Trust In The Lord

Trust in the Lord with all your heart. (Proverbs 3:5)

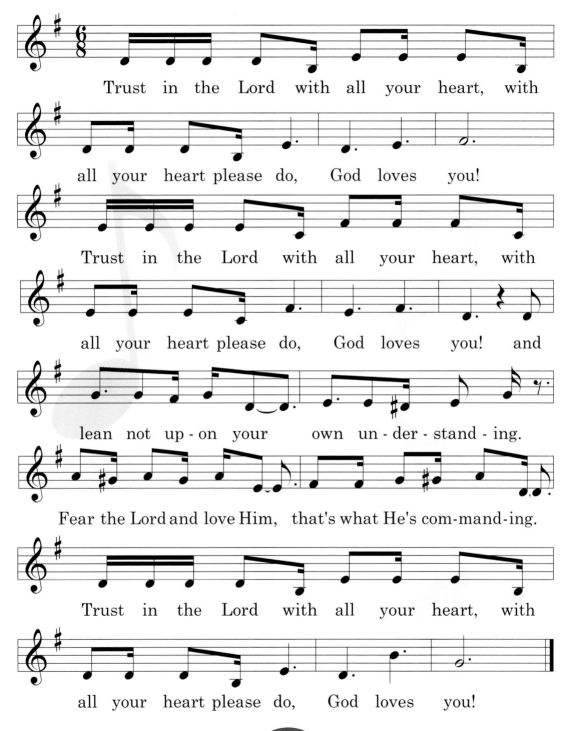

Trust in the Lord with all your heart, with

all your heart please do, God loves you!

Trust in the Lord with all your heart, with

all your heart please do, God loves you! and

lean not up-on your own un-der-stand-ing.

Fear the Lord and love Him, that's what He's com-mand-ing.

Trust in the Lord with all your heart, with

all your heart please do, God loves you!

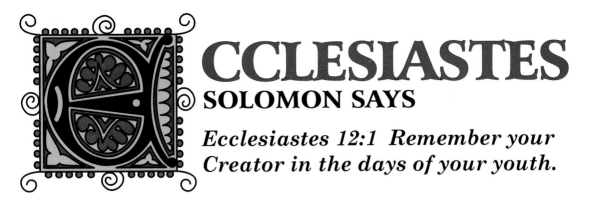

ECCLESIASTES
SOLOMON SAYS

Ecclesiastes 12:1 Remember your Creator in the days of your youth.

Solomon the Preacher was the son of David and king in Jerusalem. In the book of Ecclesiastes, he gives us many verses of wisdom.

There is a right time to do everything.
A right time to plant in the spring,
A right time to pull up the plant in the fall;
A right time to laugh, and a time to be silent;
A right time to build a building, and a time to tear it down;
A right time to search for that which is lost,
*   and a time to stop looking;*
A right time to speak, and a time to keep silent.
Part of being wise is choosing to do things at the right time.

There is nothing better than serving the Lord, for this will lead to happiness. Every day is a gift from the Lord to you. Enjoy the days you are given.

Life isn't fair sometimes, so do not be discouraged when you see mean people lying or cheating without being caught. The Lord knows what they are doing and someday they will be judged.

And whatever it is that you choose to do, do it the very best you can. Work to please the Lord and He will bless you. Don't be lazy. Sow your seeds in the morning and in the evening. For you never know which work will be successful. Don't give up.

Finally, don't wait until you are old before you start serving the Lord. Serve Him now while you are young and alive with energy. Serve the Lord with gladness. Respect the Lord and always keep His commandments; for this is what we are supposed to do.

Affirmation: I will serve the Lord while I am young!

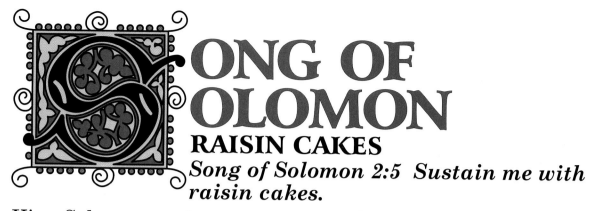

SONG OF SOLOMON

RAISIN CAKES

Song of Solomon 2:5 Sustain me with raisin cakes.

King Solomon wrote many songs and poems for the wife he loved. He knew that his marriage vows were very serious and that lasting love requires a little work. So he worked at it. He knew that romantic love can draw two people together, but only the Lord can make it last forever. Therefore, Solomon wrote this simple poem to his wife.

How beautiful you are, my darling.
Oh, how beautiful are your eyes.
You are like a lily among thorns
    compared to other girls.
Strengthen me with raisin cakes,
Refresh me with apples,
For I have grown tired
    and I love sitting with you.
How beautiful you are, my darling.
Oh, how beautiful are your eyes.

Affirmation:
The Lord will
sustain me!

204

Raisin Cakes

Sustain me with raisin cakes. (Song of Solomon 2:5)

O Lord sus - tain me

with rai - sin cakes.

O Lord sus - tain me

with rai - sin cakes.

O Lord sus - tain me

with rai - sin cakes.

Verse II: O Lord, when I marry, sustain our home.
Verse III: O Lord, won't you bless me with a love so true.

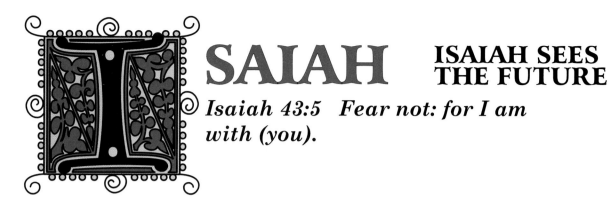

ISAIAH

ISAIAH SEES THE FUTURE

Isaiah 43:5   Fear not: for I am with (you).

The nation of Israel had once again fallen deep into sin. They had rebelled against the Lord and chosen a wicked way of living.

There arose a prophet of God named Isaiah who came to proclaim God's coming judgments on Israel and upon the whole earth. He told them that God would not allow their sin to go unpunished.

"Clean your minds," Isaiah proclaimed. "Make yourselves a holy people. Repent and stop doing evil things. Learn to do good! And though your sins be as scarlet, they shall be washed whiter than snow."

Isaiah taught the people to stop calling bad things good, and good things bad. "Have faith," he said, "and follow the Lord even when His ways are unclear to you. Respect the Lord and trust in Him. For there is no salvation in knowing about God. You must pray and spend time with God. And know this above all things: God loves you," he said, "and though we are very small, God cares for us."

Isaiah was a prophet, a person with a message from God. Isaiah's message was not only about the past and the present, but also about the future. Hundreds of years before Jesus was born, Isaiah wrote of His birth and His death. God had allowed him to see into the future.

"For unto us a child (Jesus) is born, unto us a son is given. And He alone will establish a kingdom. And He will be called Wonderful Counselor, Mighty God, Everlasting Father, The Prince Of Peace."

Isaiah also wrote of Jesus' death:

(Jesus) was despised and rejected by men. He took upon himself our sins and sorrows. He was pierced because of the sinful deeds we had done. He took the punishment we deserved and because of this, we are forgiven. For everyone is guilty of sinning, but Jesus has been punished in our place ... though He had done nothing wrong.

The Lord spoke many wonderful things through the prophet Isaiah.

Affirmation: I will serve Jesus, the Prince of Peace!

Praise Him 'Til The Sun Goes Down

Fear not: for I am with (you). (Isaiah 43:5)

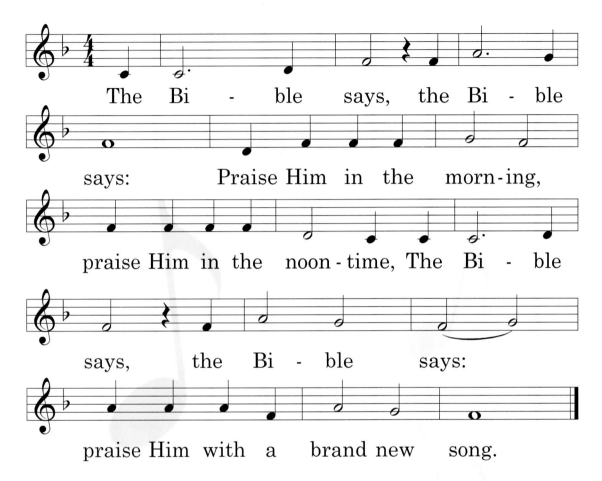

The Bi - ble says, the Bi - ble

says: Praise Him in the   morn-ing,

praise Him in the noon-time, The Bi - ble

says,   the Bi - ble   says:

praise Him with a   brand new   song.

Verse II: The Bible says, the Bible says: You will be my witness. You will be my witness.
The Bible says, the Bible says: You will be my witness today.
Verse III: The Bible says, the Bible says: Fear not for I am with you. Fear not for I am
with you. The Bible says, the Bible says: Fear not for I am with you today.

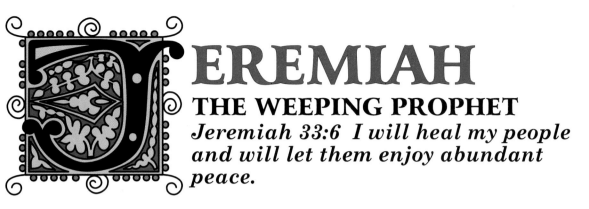

JEREMIAH
THE WEEPING PROPHET
Jeremiah 33:6 I will heal my people and will let them enjoy abundant peace.

The prophet Jeremiah grew up in a wealthy family during the time of King Josiah's revival. Men and women everywhere were turning away from evil and coming back to God's way. But as time passed, the people drifted back to their evil ways. Jeremiah was called to preach when he was very young. He saw his people worshiping idols and disobeying the law of the Lord. So he cried, "Repent!" with tears running down his cheeks. He was soon nicknamed "the weeping prophet."

Here are ten of Jeremiah's teachings:

On being too young:
God will never ask you to do something without giving you the strength and ability to do it. So never worry about being too young or too old. If God calls you, obey Him.

On being obedient:
Disobeying the Lord can become a very bad habit. If we know the right thing to do and disobey anyway, God will be very disappointed in us. If we know the right way to live and follow leaders who are preaching lies, God will be very disappointed in us. Choose to obey God.

211

On prayer:

Ask God to show you the right way, for God's way leads to peace. Pray about life's decisions. God will direct your steps if you ask Him.

On bad habits:

If you make sinful deeds a habit, very soon it may be hard to change your ways. Can a leopard change his spots?

On peer pressure:
It is always better to sit alone than to sit with people who are mocking God. Don't let bad people change you.

On trusting God:
It is good for boys and girls to trust in the Lord. Believe that God will do what He says He will do. You will be blessed.

On the nearness of God:
God is very near to you at all times. He knows your name and He knows what you are feeling. God is near.

On God's power:
Nothing is too hard or impossible for God. Ask God to help you with your troubles each day.

On being thankful:
Give thanks unto the Lord for all He is doing for you. There is much goodness to come!

On being brave:
Do not be afraid, for God is with you. He walks with you, so call on His name and He will hear.

Affirmation: I will ask God to help me each day!

I Will

I will heal my people and will let them enjoy
abundant peace. (Jeremiah 33:6)

I will, I will,

I will re-store you to health.

I will, I will,

I will heal your wounds.

I will, I will,

I will heal my peo - ple.

I will, I will

let them en-joy a-bun-dant peace.

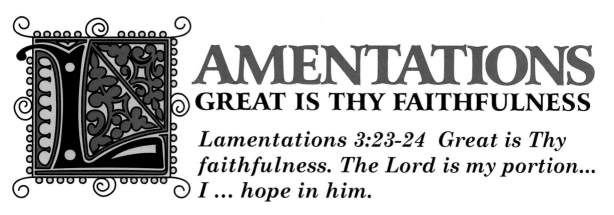

LAMENTATIONS

GREAT IS THY FAITHFULNESS

Lamentations 3:23-24 Great is Thy faithfulness. The Lord is my portion... I ... hope in him.

When Jeremiah was very old, he wrote a second book called Lamentations. In this book he is telling future generations what can happen if they turn away from God. Jerusalem is controlled by Babylon, thus Jeremiah writes with a broken heart.

"Today, there is no one in the streets of Jerusalem. It was once full of people going here to there, but now they are no longer free; they are imprisoned like slaves. Her new masters are enjoying themselves while Jerusalem suffers hardships. The Lord has brought this on because their sin was so great.

As the people remembered all of the many blessings God had given them in the past, they weep. For they did not consider how God would repay them for such sinfulness. Now there was no comfort. Even their churches had been taken over by idol worshipers.

They remembered a time when food was plentiful, now they were hungry. Even the children were begging for bread. The enemy had prevailed.

'Why did we rebel?' they asked.

'Look what it has lead to. The Lord no longer protects us and we are brought down by idol worshipers. How could we forget that God controls the outcome of every battle? Because of our sin, He has handed us over to the enemy.'

But yet I still remember this one thing: Hope. Because of the Lord's great faithfulness and love, we are not dead. His mercies never fail, they are new every morning. The Lord will be our hope. Great is Your faithfulness. Let us return to the Lord. Let us repent. Let us call upon the Lord. Let us be restored, O Lord, we pray You will give us a second chance!"

Affirmation: I will call upon the Lord who is faithful!

Great Is Thy Faithfulness

Great is Thy faithfulness. The Lord is my portion...
I ... hope in him. (Lamentations 3:23-24)

Great is Your faith - ful - ness.

Great is Your faith - ful - ness.

God is my por - tion and

I hope in him. God is so

good to those who wait

for Him. God is so

good to those who pray to Him.

Verse I: Great is Thy faithfulness. Great is Thy faithfulness. Morning by morning new mercies I see. All I have needed Thy hand has provided. Great is Thy faithfulness, Lord unto me.

EZEKIEL

DRY BONES

Ezekiel 34:26 There will be showers of blessing.

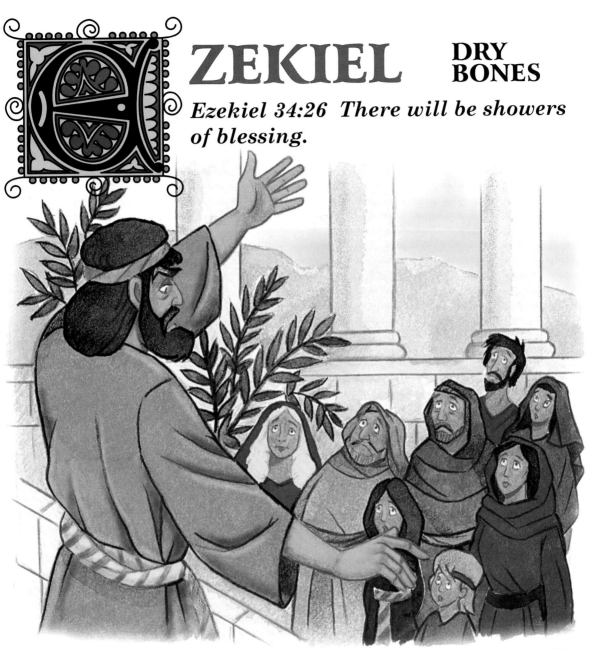

When Ezekiel the prophet arrived on the scene, the Israelite nation was held captive in Babylon. At the very same time Jeremiah was preaching near Jerusalem. God called Ezekiel to preach a message of hope. "God has not forgotten you!" he shouted. "God does not want anyone to die with sin in their lives. Repent!"

One night, God caused Ezekiel to have a strange dream. Ezekiel was taken to the middle of a large valley. This valley was full of bones. God walked with Ezekiel back and forth through the valley. There was no end to the old dry bones.

Then the Lord asked, "Can these bones live?"
Ezekiel answered, "I don't know, Lord. Only You know!"
Then the Lord spoke again, "Ezekiel, say to these bones 'You will live. The Lord will breathe life into you and you will come to life. Then you will know that I am the Lord.'"

Ezekiel obeyed the Lord. As he was speaking, there came a noise; a rattling sound. The bones were coming back together. And as they came together, the Lord caused them to be covered with skin.

But there was no breath in them yet. Then the Lord said, "Ezekiel, tell them the Lord God says to breathe!" As soon as Ezekiel spoke the word, breath entered their bodies and they came to life. They stood up on their feet, a vast army.

Then the Lord spoke again. "Ezekiel, here's what this vision means: My people think there is no hope. They believe they are cut off from Me and dead just like those dry bones. Tell them that the Lord is going to bring them back to life and return them once again to the promised land."

Ezekiel proclaimed the message, "Dry bones can live. All things are possible with God."

Affirmation: All things are possible with God!

Showers of Blessing

There will be showers of blessing. (Ezekiel 34:26)

There will be show-ers of bless-ing

fall-ing on you; show-ers of bless-ing

fall-ing on you; show-ers of bless-ing

fall - ing on you. (thunder/rain) So

let the bless - ings fall.

Verse I: The prophet Ezekiel had a dream.   Tell us, Ezekiel, what
does it mean? Dry bones can live; know this is true, showers of blessing
will fall on you.

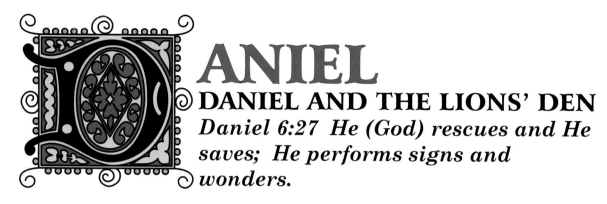

DANIEL

DANIEL AND THE LIONS' DEN

Daniel 6:27 He (God) rescues and He saves; He performs signs and wonders.

In the third year of the reign of King Jehoiakim, Jerusalem was attacked and defeated by King Nebuchadnezzar of Babylon. The Babylonians carried off the cups and other vessels from the holy temple. They began using them in their own idol worship. The king then ordered the smartest and most handsome young men of Israel to be brought to his palace. There they would stay for three years being trained to serve the king. One of these young men was a Jewish boy named Daniel.

Each day Daniel was given a portion of royal food and wine, but he refused to eat it. He chose instead to eat vegetables and drink water. In doing so, he did not break the Jewish law.

When the three years of training ended, all of the young men were presented to King Nebuchadnezzar. Daniel was by far the smartest and most handsome of them all. That day, he entered the king's service. He served for many years until Nebuchadnezzar died and his grandson Belshazzar became king.

The Lord gave Daniel the gift of interpreting dreams. On many occasions, Daniel was able to interpret the king's dreams and he soon became well-known as a very wise man of God. One night, Belshazzar gave a great party. A thousand guests were there. The king gave orders to bring out the gold and silver cups his father had stolen from the Jewish temple years ago. They began pouring wine into these holy cups while they praised their false gods. The Lord was very angry. Suddenly, a mysterious hand appeared in the room and began writing strange words on the palace wall.

The king collapsed with fear. He called out, "If anyone can tell me what this means, speak now and I will make you third in command of Babylon." All of the king's wise men tried, but they could not read the message. Then the queen spoke, "There is a man who walks with the God of Israel in your kingdom. His name is Daniel. Call for him. He will tell you what the writing means."

So Daniel was brought before the king. "Can you read this? Tell me!" demanded the king. "Yes, O king. God has given me the ability to read it," answered Daniel. "It says you have not honored the living God, but mocked Him."

Daniel was made third in command of Babylon. But that night Belshazzar, king of Babylon was killed and Darius the Mede took over the kingdom.

King Darius hand-picked 120 princes to rule his new kingdom. He then selected three presidents to oversee the princes. Of these three, Daniel became the most important. The other presidents and governors were jealous that Daniel had been honored in this way, so they plotted against him.

MENE MENE TEKEL PARSIN

They went to the king as a group and said, "O King Darius, all of us have agreed that you should make a new law this day; a law that will unite the kingdom. The new law would make it a crime for anyone to pray to any god or man but you, O King, for the next thirty days. And if anyone should break the new law, they would be thrown into the lions' den." So King Darius agreed and it was put into writing.

Now when Daniel heard about the new law, he went upstairs to his room, got down on his knees, and prayed, just as he had done before. When the princes and governors found Daniel praying, they ran to the king and said, "Daniel has broken your new law, O King. He must be punished. Throw him to the lions!" Darius did not want to harm Daniel, but these evil men had tricked him. So King Darius gave the order, "Put Daniel into the lions' den."

They took Daniel to the lions' den and threw him in. Then King Darius spoke to Daniel, "May the God whom you serve rescue you!" Then they sealed the den shut and the king returned to the palace.

At dawn, the king arose from a sleepless night and hurried to the den. "Daniel," he cried, "are you alive? Has your God rescued you from the lions?" Daniel answered, "My God has sent an angel who shut the mouths of the lions. They have not hurt me, nor have I done any wrong to you, O King."

"Pull him up!" shouted the king. Then, at the king's command, those men who had falsely accused Daniel were thrown into the den of lions. Then King Darius sent a letter throughout the kingdom which read: All the people of the kingdom must fear and respect the God of Daniel, for He is the living God who rescued and saved Daniel from the lions.

Daniel loved the Lord and faithfully served Him.

Affirmation: I will honor the living God!

He's Got The Whole World In His Hands

He (God) rescues and He saves; He performs signs and wonders. (Daniel 6:27)

He's got the whole world

in His hands. He's got the whole world

in His hands. He's got the whole world

in His hands. He's got the

whole world in His hands.

Verse II: He had Daniel and the lions in His hands. He's got the whole world in His hands.

Verse III: He is the living God. We're in His hands. He's got the whole world in His hands.

Verse IV: He performs signs and wonders with His hands. He's got the whole world in His hands.

Verse V: He rescues and He saves. We're in His hands. He's got the whole world in His hands.

HOSEA

SOW THE WIND

Hosea 14:9 For the ways of the Lord are right, (let's) walk in them.

"You sow the wind and reap the whirlwind," shouted Hosea the prophet to the people of Israel. For they had once again forgotten the Lord. But wise Hosea knew how sin was working in their lives. Little sins were now causing big problems. Husbands were unfaithful to wives, children were disobedient to parents, and idol worship was everywhere. But God, in his loving kindness, called Hosea to preach, "O Israel, stop sinning and change your ways!"

He knew that sin always pays back more than you put into it. "The blessing of God will soon be gone if you continue to be unfaithful," he said. But the people would not listen. The armies of Assyria came and conquered Israel on a day they least expected it. Now as captives they remembered Hosea's warning, "You sow the wind and reap the whirlwind. For the ways of the Lord are right." It was a very sad day in Israel.

Affirmation: I will walk in the ways of the Lord!

Walk, Walk Your Talk

For the ways of the Lord are right, (let's) walk in them.   (Hosea 14:9)

For the ways of the Lord are right, let's walk in them.

1. Walk, walk, walk, walk your talk. For the

2. walk your talk. For the ways of the Lord are right,

let's walk in them. Walk, walk, walk, walk your talk. For the

ways of the Lord are right, let's walk in them.

Walk, walk, walk, walk your talk.

Walk, walk, walk, walk, walk your talk. Walk, walk, walk, walk,

walk your talk. Walk, walk, walk, walk.

JOEL

DON'T BUG ME

Joel 2:27 I am the Lord your God,... there is no other; never again will my people be ashamed.

While Hosea preached repentance in the northern part of Israel, the prophet Joel came on the scene in Judah, the southern kingdom. His message was the same, but the situation "bugged" a lot of people.

At that time a huge black swarm of locusts had swept across the land. There were millions of creepy, crawly bugs everywhere. These locusts began eating every plant in sight In a matter of hours, all their fields were ruined. Joel announced that God had sent the locusts to humble the people and turn them back to the Lord.

"Come back to the Lord with all your heart," declared Joel. "Gather the people and pray. Praise the name of the Lord who has worked wonders for you. Then, and only then, will the Lord rid the land of these terrible bugs! Then, and only then, will He send a new blessing of food and prosperity."

The Lord promised to one day restore Israel. He warned that the things we do in this lifetime matter to God. For heaven awaits those who love and serve God now, and judgment awaits those who turn away.

Affirmation: I will love and serve the Lord!

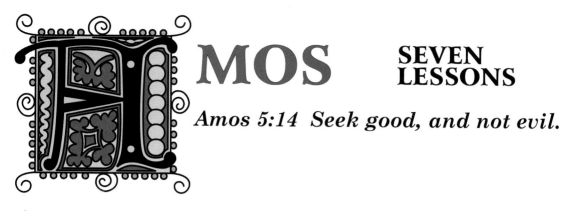

AMOS

Amos 5:14 Seek good, and not evil.

Amos was a simple farmer from a small town called Tekoa in Israel. Amos was never trained as a preacher. He worked growing sycamore figs and tended to his sheep the whole day long.

One day God gave this tenderhearted farmer a powerful message to deliver to Israel. The Israelites were enjoying great wealth, but had forgotten to give thanks to God. They were also ignoring the poor and needy. Amos traveled to Bethel where he warned the people. "God hates your sin," he shouted. "Your disobedience may cause another famine, drought, or plague. Please stop sinning!" But the people would not listen.

Amos taught the people seven important lessons we all should know:

1. *Sin causes God's heart to break because He loves us*
2. *To be God's friend, you must agree with Him and obey Him*
3. *God may send unpleasant things into our lives to keep us from sinning.*
4. *Having riches in this world is not necessarily a blessing from God.*
5. *There is coming a day when the true Word of God will not be preached.*
6. *We should seek good and not evil.*
7. *We should be preparing to meet the Lord and hear Him say, "Well done!"*

Amos ended his book with a promise from God. "I have not forgotten you, says the Lord. I will give Israel a home, and there they will stay forever."

Affirmation: I will seek good!

OBADIAH
A NATION ON TRIAL

Obadiah 1:15 (For) the day of the Lord is near.

Once there was a very small nation called Edom. Edom had been an enemy of Israel for many years. Edomites were the descendants of Esau. They had opposed King Saul and fought King David, the descendants of Jacob. So God chose the prophet Obadiah to deliver His message to Edom. "You are full of pride and selfishness, and for this you will be destroyed, says the Lord."

The Edomites laughed at Obadiah because they had a great city called Petra which was in the mountains where they thought no one could attack them. "God could never destroy our city," they jeered. It's never a good thing to mock the Lord.

The Edomites hated Israel so much that they rejoiced and celebrated every time trouble came upon God's people. How they mocked Obadiah and laughed! This angered the Lord. But in time, Obadiah's words came true. Shortly thereafter the Edomites were defeated by an invading nation. We should never laugh while others are suffering. We must always seek to help, not hurt. This is the lesson of Obadiah.

Affirmation: I will seek to help others!

JONAH

A WHALE OF A TALE

Jonah 4:2 You are a gracious and compassionate God, slow to anger and abounding in love.

One day the Lord spoke to Jonah the prophet, "Go to the city of Nineveh and tell them that God has seen their wickedness and they must stop sinning." But Jonah didn't want to go. So he decided to run away from the Lord. He boarded a sailing ship bound for Tarshish.

But the Lord knows where we are every single moment. He knew Jonah had disobeyed His command, so He sent a violent storm over the sea.

The wind roared and the waves crashed against the ship. The sailors were so afraid they began to pray to their false gods. They even threw the ship's cargo into the sea to make it float better.

But where was Jonah? He had gone below deck where he lay fast asleep! When the captain found Jonah sleeping, he shouted, "How can you sleep when we are about to be drowned? Get up and pray that your God will save us!"

The other sailors began to think that Jonah was somehow responsible for the storm, so they asked him, "Is it your fault we are in this terrible trouble? Who are you? Where are you from?" Jonah answered, "I am a Hebrew. I worship the Lord of heaven who made the sea."

"What have you done to anger Him?" they asked. "I am running away from the Lord. This storm is my fault," Jonah replied. Suddenly a giant wave crashed onto the deck as the thunder cracked louder! "What can we do to calm the raging sea?" the sailors cried. 'Throw me into the sea and it will become calm!" Jonah said.

But the men did not want Jonah to die, so they rowed even harder. But the storm grew wilder. "Forgive us, Lord," the men prayed. Then they picked Jonah up and threw him into the raging sea.
Suddenly, the sea was calm. Everything was still.

When this happened, all of the sailors made promises to serve the God of Jonah. But poor Jonah was sinking deeper and deeper below the waves until a great fish swallowed Jonah whole. There he stayed for three days.

When Jonah realized what had happened, he began to pray. "I am in deep trouble, O Lord, and yet You have saved my life. Hear my song of thanksgiving!"

As Jonah continued to pray, the giant fish was swimming toward dry land where it spit Jonah out. The Lord spoke to Jonah for the second time. "Go to Nineveh and proclaim My message of salvation." This time, Jonah went straight to Nineveh!

For three days Jonah told everyone in Nineveh, "Repent, or God will destroy this city in 40 days!" When the people heard Jonah's voice, they knew he was preaching the truth. All of Nineveh believed God and declared a city-wide day of prayer and fasting. They turned from their evil ways and blessed the God of Jonah.

Affirmation: I will obey the Lord!

MICAH

POOR LITTLE RICH BOY

Micah 4:2 Let us go up to the mountain of the Lord ... He will teach us his ways.

Micah was a great prophet of the Lord who stood up for the poor in Israel. Micah preached against rich rulers who were stealing land from the poor and not listening to their cries for help. Micah taught the people, "Each of us must do what is right before God. We must show kindness and forgive one another. Turn to the Lord and tell Him all the things you have done wrong, then God will forgive you. The Lord will be your light."

Affirmation: I will show kindness to others!

Climb Sunshine Mountain

Let us go up to the mountain of the Lord . . . He will teach us his ways. (Micah 4:2)

Let us go up to the moun-tain, the

moun - tain of the Lord.

Let us go up to the moun - tain,

sing in one ac - cord. He will

teach us his ways, Oh praise Him,

Look to God on high.

Let us go up to the moun-tain, you and I.

Verse II: Climb, climb up sunshine mountain heav'nly breezes blow. Climb, climb up sunshine mountain, faces all aglow. Turn, turn from sin and sorrow, look to God on high. Climb, climb up sunshine mountain, you and I.

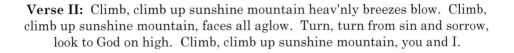

NAHUM
NO TRACE OF NINEVEH

Nahum 1:7 The Lord is good ... He cares for those who trust in him.

One hundred years after Jonah had preached in Nineveh, the Lord called Nahum the prophet to that great city. The people there no longer worshiped the God of Israel. They had returned to their wicked ways with false gods and idol worship.

Nahum called out, "People of Nineveh, you must stop sinning. Repent and return to the Lord! If you don't, you will be destroyed and no trace of Nineveh will remain. Remember the Lord is good and He knows those who take refuge in Him."

The people laughed at Nahum and would not return to the Lord. Soon, the Babylonians came and destroyed Nineveh just as Nahum had warned. We must obey the word of God, for it guides and directs us as people and as a nation.

Affirmation: I will tell everyone the Lord is good!

The Lord Is Good

The Lord is good . . . He cares for those
who trust in him. (Nahum 1:7)

The Lord is ver - y good to me. The

Lord is ver-y good to me. The

Lord is ver-y good to me. He

cares for you and me.

Verse I: The Lord is slow to anger. The Lord is powerful. The mountains quake before him; He rebukes the sea. What a mighty God we serve, let's serve Him faithfully.

Verse II: The Lord will guide His people. The Lord will take care of us. O how the earth does tremble when the Lord is near. The world and all who live in it, this message they should hear.

Chorus II: He cares for those who trust in Him. He cares for those who trust in Him. He cares for those who trust in Him. He cares for you and me.

250

HABAKKUK
TWO QUESTIONS

Habakkuk 2:4 The just shall live by ... faith.

Habakkuk the prophet teaches a great lesson in his very short book: God always does things at just the right time.

Habakkuk had called out to God with a question. "How long will You allow these sinful and hardhearted people to go unpunished? For evil abounds, and good men and women are being unfairly treated." The Lord answered and said, "This very minute I am strengthening the Babylonian army. They will sweep across this land and punish these proud people. But the just shall live by faith."

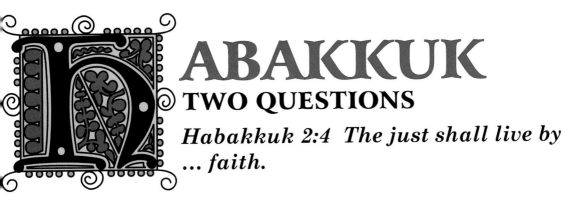

Habakkuk was shocked and asked God a second question, "How can You use an evil nation like Babylon to accomplish good?" Then the Lord told Habakkuk that someday everyone would know God. Habakkuk praised the Lord for teaching him these great truths.

Then the Lord spoke, "Who I use to bring about good upon the earth is not important. What is important is faith. Each person must believe in Me by faith."

Affirmation:
I will believe in
God by faith!

The Just Shall Live By Faith

The just shall live by ... faith.   (Habakkuk 2:4)

The just shall live by faith. The

just shall live by faith.

We de-clare a verse to share: The

just shall live by faith.

Verse II: O friend, have faith in God. O friend, have faith in God.
We declare a verse to share: O friend, have faith in God.
Verse III: Increase our faith, O Lord. Increase our faith, O Lord.
We declare a verse to share: Increase our faith, O Lord.
Verse IV: We walk by faith, not sight. We walk by faith, not
sight. We declare a verse to share: We walk by faith, not sight.
Verse V: The just shall live by faith. The just shall live by faith.
We declare a verse to share: The just shall live by faith.

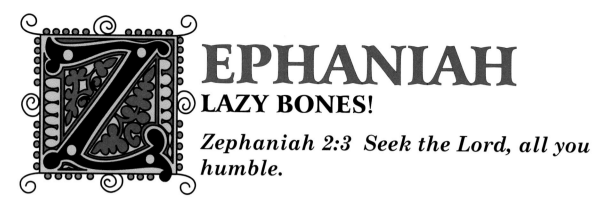

ZEPHANIAH
LAZY BONES!

Zephaniah 2:3 Seek the Lord, all you humble.

During the reign of King Josiah, God raised up a great prophet named Zephaniah. During this time the people of Israel had become very selfish and had fallen into idol worship and astrology. But their sin of laziness angered the Lord greatly. They no longer cared about the things of God; things like prayer and worship. "God isn't going to do anything good or bad," they said. "We'll do what we want." They totally forgot about the Lord.

Zephaniah continued to warn these "lazy bones" of God's coming judgement by saying, "Don't be lazy, let's seek the Lord all you humble of the earth."

But not everyone in Israel had "lazy bones." There was a small group or "remnant" of faithful believers to whom God made a promise. "Though you have been mocked and made fun of, you will soon be blessed!" And God keeps His promises. He saved this remnant and there was soon a great revival because of their faithfulness. Our God always keeps His promises.

Affirmation: I will keep my promises!

HAGGAI

OK ... BACK TO WORK!

Haggai 2:4-5 I am with you, declares the Lord ... My spirit is (abiding) in your midst.

One day King Cyrus of Babylon allowed the captive Israelites to return to their homeland, Jerusalem. When they arrived, they started rebuilding the Lord's temple. But soon they grew tired and discouraged and the work stopped.

God sent a prophet named Haggai to Zerubbabel, the governor of Judah. The Lord says, "Why are the people building fine houses for themselves, yet my house stands in ruin? Go to the mountains and bring back many trees and begin working on my house. Until you have done this, I will not bless the work of your hands."

Zerubbabel and the people obeyed the voice of the Lord. They began working on the temple. The Lord was pleased and promised to make this temple even greater than Solomon's temple. "One day," said the Lord, "the desire of all nations (who is Jesus) will come and His glory will fill this temple."

"Though in times past I stopped your work from succeeding, from this day on I will bless you." Five years later the temple of the Lord was finished and God was very pleased.

Affirmation: I will serve my church faithfully!

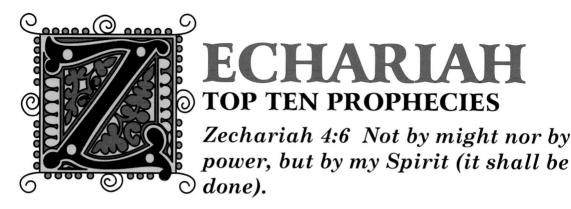

ZECHARIAH
TOP TEN PROPHECIES

Zechariah 4:6 Not by might nor by power, but by my Spirit (it shall be done).

During the time that Haggai was preaching in Jerusalem, a man named Zechariah came on the scene. His message was the same: "God's work must come first," proclaimed Zechariah. "We must rebuild the temple now."

But Zechariah also had a very special message regarding our coming savior. His book spoke about Jesus' coming more than any other book in the Bible. Here are ten prophecies from this wonderful book.

1. *The Messiah will enter Jerusalem as a King. (9:9)*
2. *He will save His people. (9:9)*
3. *He will be riding on a donkey. (9:9)*
4. *He will proclaim peace to the nations. (9:10)*
5. *His kingdom will cover the entire earth. (9:10)*
6. *He will be sold for 30 pieces of silver. (11:12)*
7. *His body will be pierced because of our sins. (12:10)*
8. *He will be a first-born son. (12:10)*
9. *His blood will cleanse us of sin. (13:1)*
10. *That someday He will return for a second time. (14:1)*

❧ ❦

Does this sound like Jesus? Of course it does! The Lord taught the people that we build successful lives, "Not by might nor by power, but by my Spirit says the Lord." Zechariah was truly a man of God.

Affirmation: I will follow the Holy Spirit!

MALACHI
HARDHEARTED QUESTIONS

Malachi 3:6 For I, the Lord, do not change.

The Word of the Lord came again to Israel through a man named Malachi. Malachi asked the people seven tough questions. The answers to these questions would show how hardhearted they had become.

Question 1: I hear you ask, "How has the Lord shown His love to us?" He's shown His love by protecting you from your enemies and providing you with food and shelter.

Question 2: I see your sons honor their fathers, and servants their masters, but where is the honor due the Lord's name? You honor yourselves more than the Lord.

Question 3: *I hear you ask, "Why is the Lord angry with us?"* Because you have given your worst to Him and the very best to yourselves.

Question 4: *I hear you ask, "Why does the Lord ignore our offerings?"* He ignores them because you have been unfaithful to your wives and husbands.

Question 5: *You rob the Lord and ask, "How do we rob Him?"* You rob Him by not bringing your tithes and offerings to the temple. If you will do this, He will throw open the floodgates of heaven and pour out so much blessing that you will not have room enough for it.

Question 6: *I hear you ask, "What do we gain by serving the Lord?"* You gain eternal life. Your name will be written on the scroll of remembrance.

Question 7: *I have heard you say things about the Lord that are untrue. Then you ask, "What did we say Lord?"* You said there is no reason to serve God. Evildoers still prosper and we do not. But a day is coming when He will judge the wicked and they will not escape.

Affirmation: I will give an offering to the Lord!

God Is Light

For I, the Lord, do not change.   (Malachi 3:6)

For I the Lord, do not change.

God is light. God is light.

For I the Lord, do not change.

God is light, God is light.

Verse II: In Him there is no darkness. God is light, God is
light. In Him there is no darkness. God is light, God is light.
Verse III: Don't be afraid, just believe. God is light. God is
light. Don't be afraid, just believe. God is light, God is light.

"Let the little children
come to me."

The **NEW TESTAMENT**

GABRIEL'S VISIT

Now this is how the birth of Jesus Christ came about. In the
days when Herod was king of Judea, there lived a priest
named Zacharias. He had a wonderful wife named
Elizabeth. They had grown old together but had no children.

One day Zacharias was in the temple preparing an offering to the Lord when suddenly, an angel appeared before him.

Zacharias was afraid! "Do not be afraid, for God has heard your prayers. Soon you and Elizabeth will have a baby boy. You are to name him John, for he will be a great man of God. Because of his preaching many will repent and turn back to God. He will prepare the way for the coming of the Lord."

Zacharias said to the angel, "How can this be true? I am too old to have children and so is my wife."

"I am Gabriel, a messenger sent by God to tell you this wonderful news. But since you have not believed me, you shall be unable to speak until all of these things have happened." Then as quickly as he had come, Gabriel disappeared.

Outside the temple, the people were waiting for Zacharias wondering what was keeping him. Finally, he came out unable to speak. He used sign language to try to tell them what had happened. They thought he had seen a vision!

Finally, a silent Zacharias returned home. Soon Elizabeth discovered that she was going to have a baby, just as Gabriel had said.

Now sometime later, Gabriel was sent by God to the city of Nazareth to visit a young woman named Mary. She was engaged to marry a carpenter named Joseph.

But before their wedding day, Gabriel came to her and said, "Hello favored one, the Lord is with you!" Mary had never heard such a greeting before and wondered, "What does it mean?"

Gabriel spoke again, "Do not be afraid Mary, for I have a message for you from the Lord. You are going to have a baby boy and you shall call His name Jesus. He will be great and will be called the Son of God, and His kingdom will have no end!"

Mary was confused. "How can this be?" she asked. "I have no husband yet."

Gabriel answered, "Nothing is impossible with God. Even Elizabeth your relative is going to have a baby, though she is very old. For nothing will be impossible with God."

"I am the servant of the Lord," said Mary. "Let all that you have said be done in my life." And in an instant, the angel was gone.

Mary couldn't wait to tell Elizabeth about Gabriel's visit.
She left Nazareth at once and hurried through the hills of
Judah. When she arrived at Zacharias' house, she hurried
inside and called, "Elizabeth! It is me, Mary." When
Elizabeth heard Mary's voice, her baby jumped inside her
and the Spirit of God filled her. "How blessed you are, Mary,
to be the mother of my Lord."

Mary wondered, "How could Elizabeth know about the baby Jesus? I haven't told her yet. I am happy," said Mary, "because God is my Lord and Savior. Holy is His name." Mary stayed with Elizabeth for three months and then she returned home.

Affirmation: Nothing is impossible with God!

JOHN IS BORN *Luke 1:57-66*

Time passed and soon Elizabeth's baby was born. Their friends and church leaders wanted to name the child Zacharias, like his father. But Elizabeth said, "No, his name will be John."

"You can't call him John," they said. "Let's ask Zacharias what the child's name will be." On a tablet Zacharias wrote, "His name is John." At that very moment, Zacharias could once again speak. And oh, how he praised the Lord! "This must be a very special child," the people said, "for the hand of the Lord is upon him."

Affirmation: I will praise the Lord!

JESUS IS BORN

Matthew 1:21 And you shall call His name Jesus, for He will save His people from their sins.

When Mary told Joseph all of the things that had happened to her and Elizabeth, he was very confused. But one night as he slept, an angel of the Lord appeared to him in a dream and said, "Mary is a good woman. Do not put her away. Take her as your wife, for her baby is a miracle baby that God himself has given her."

"And you shall call His name Jesus, for He will save His people from their sins."

When Joseph awoke from his dream, he did exactly what the angel asked him to do. He took Mary as his wife and he never doubted again.

Now it came about that the Roman king, Caesar Augustus, wanted to know how many people were living in his kingdom. So everyone, including Joseph and Mary, had to return to their own city to be counted. Mary was ready to have her baby, but still they made the journey from Nazareth to the city of David which is called Bethlehem.

When they arrived in Bethlehem, it was very crowded. Mary was ready to give birth, and though Joseph looked everywhere for a room, there was none to be found. Finally, Joseph and Mary came to a stable where sheep and livestock were kept. There Jesus Christ, the Son of God, was born. And Mary wrapped Him in swaddling clothes and laid Him in a manger, which is a feeding box. There, under the stars of Bethlehem, the baby Jesus slept.

Nearby, there was a group of shepherds keeping watch over their flocks of sheep.

Suddenly, an angel of the Lord appeared before them and the darkness was filled with light! The shepherds were so afraid!

Then the angel spoke. "Do not be afraid, for I bring you good news of a great joy! Today in Bethlehem, your Savior is born who is Christ the Lord."

"Come and see the Lord! You will know it is He when you find the baby wrapped in swaddling clothes and lying in a manger."

Then suddenly, many angels appeared before them, praising God and saying, "Glory to God in the highest. And on earth, peace among men with whom He is pleased."

When the angels departed, the shepherds said, "Let's go to Bethlehem right now to see this thing that has happened." So they hurried into town and found their way to Mary and Joseph. And just as the angel had said, they found Christ the Lord lying in a manger.

Now when they had seen all this, they told everyone about Jesus and the appearance of angels. The shepherds went back to their flocks, praising God all the way!

Affirmation: I love Jesus!

O Come And Worship Him

We have come to worship Him! (Matthew 2:2)

Verse I: Where is He born King of the Jews? We've

seen His star in the east as it moves.

We have come to wor-ship Him,

O come and wor-ship Him. Chorus: O

star of won-der, star of night,

star with roy-al beau-ty bright.

West-ward lead-ing, still pro-ceed-ing,

guide us to Thy per-fect light.

Verse II: We three Kings of Orient are, bearing gifts we travel so far. Field and fountain, moor and mountain, following yonder star.

Zacharias and Elizabeth's baby boy grew to be a very rugged man. He became known as John the Baptist and he lived and preached in the desert. For food he ate locusts and wild honey, and he wore a coat of camel hair.

His message was very simple, "Repent! Stop doing evil things and return to God's ways, for the kingdom of heaven is coming soon."

Many people would come to John and be baptized in the Jordan River. They would tell God how sorry they were for not obeying Him and promised to live for Him.

Then one day as John stood in the Jordan River, he saw Jesus walking towards him to be baptized. John knew that Jesus had never sinned and did not need to be baptized. So John said, "It is I who needs to be baptized by You. Why do You come to me?"

Jesus replied, "It is important that you baptize Me now. By doing this, we show others the right thing to do."

When Jesus came up out of the water, the heavens opened, and the Spirit of God came down upon Him like a dove. Then a voice came from heaven saying, "This is My son. I love Him and I am very pleased with Him."

MATTHEW
THE PRINCIPLES OF JESUS

THE BEATITUDES
Matthew 5:3 Blessed are the poor in spirit, for theirs is the kingdom of heaven.

Jesus began His ministry near the Sea of Galilee. There He began telling everyone the good news of God's coming kingdom. He healed every kind of disease and sickness. The people loved Jesus. Every day the crowds grew bigger and bigger, so Jesus went up on a mountainside where there was plenty of room for everyone to gather. There He sat down and began to teach the people.

"Blessed are the poor in spirit, for theirs is the kingdom of heaven. Blessed are the ones who mourn, for they will be comforted. Blessed are the meek, for they will inherit the earth. Blessed are the pure in heart, for they will see God. Blessed are the peacemakers, for they will be the sons of God."

Jesus went on to say that we are to be happy when people say unkind or untrue things about us. "Rejoice and be happy," He said, "because you will have a great reward one day in the kingdom of heaven."

Affirmation: I will be happy in Jesus!

The Beatitudes

Blessed are the poor in spirit, for theirs is the kingdom of heaven. Blessed are those who mourn, for they will be comforted. Blessed are the meek in spirit, for they will inherit the earth. Blessed are the pure in heart, for they will see God. Blessed are the peacemakers for they will be called Sons of God. (Matthew 5:3)

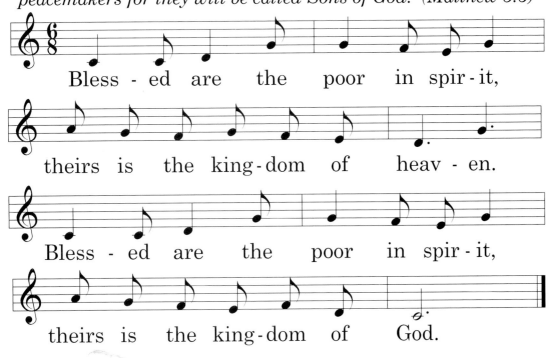

Bless - ed are the poor in spir - it,

theirs is the king-dom of heav - en.

Bless - ed are the poor in spir - it,

theirs is the king-dom of God.

Verse II: Blessed are the ones who mourn, they will be comforted.
Verse III: Blessed are the meek in spirit they will inherit the earth.
Verse IV: Blessed are the pure in heart, they will see God.
Verse V: Blessed are the peacemakers, they will be Sons of God. Blessed are the peacemakers, call them the Sons of God.

SALT AND LIGHT
Matthew 5:13-16

Jesus said that we are the salt of the earth, and real salt always makes people very thirsty. And when you're thirsty, you want a drink of water. Jesus told the people that we're supposed to be very salty and cause people who see us and hear us to want to know more about Jesus; to make them thirsty for God's Word. He said that if we lose our saltiness, we can't make people thirsty.

Jesus also said, "You are the light of the world." When people walk in the light, they can see all the dangerous things that might have hurt them if they stumbled in the darkness. God's Word is like a light. So when we share our light and tell others about Jesus, we brighten their lives. We help them see Satan's stumbling blocks.

But if we hide our lights under a bowl and tell no one that Jesus lives in our hearts, our friends and family may never see Jesus, and fall down in the darkness.

Be a light!

Affirmation: I will be a light!

THE LORD'S PRAYER

Matthew 6:9 Our Father which art in heaven, Hallowed be thy name.

Matthew was a disciple of Jesus. As they traveled together, he would write down what Jesus taught. Matthew writes: "Jesus said that there is a right way to pray and a wrong way to pray. We should not say our prayers in front of people just to make them think we're good. This is a wrong reason to pray.

When we pray, we should go into our room, close the door, and pray to our heavenly Father in secret. God promises to answer this kind of prayer by rewarding us openly. Jesus said, when you pray, use this example:

"Our Father, which art in heaven
Hallowed be Thy name.
Thy kingdom come, Thy will be done

on earth as it is in heaven.
Give us this day our daily bread.
Forgive us our debts as we forgive
our debtors. And lead us not
into temptation, but deliver
us from evil. For Thine is the
kingdom, the power and the
glory forever and ever."

The Lord's Prayer

Our Father, which art in heaven, hallowed be Thy name. Thy kingdom come,
Thy will be done on earth as it is in heaven. Give us this day our daily bread.
And lead us not into temptation, but deliver us from evil. For Thine is the
kingdom, the power and the glory forever and ever. (Matthew 6:9)

Our   Fath-er,   which   art   in   Hea-ven,

hal-low-ed be Thy   name.   Our Fath-er, which

art   in   Hea-ven,   hal-low-ed   be   Thy

name.   Thy   king - dom   come,   Thy

will   be done   on   earth as   it   is   in

hea-ven.   Thy   king - dom   come,   Thy

will be done   on   earth as it is in   hea-ven.

Bridge: Give us this day our daily bread. Give us this day our daily bread.
Verse II: And lead us not into temptation but deliver us from evil. For Thine is the kingdom,
power and glory forever and ever.

DO NOT WORRY
Matthew 6:25-34

"Look at the birds flying through the air," Jesus said. "They do not plant gardens to get food, nor do they pick corn or gather the seeds they eat. Yet, your Heavenly Father feeds them. So do not worry about what you will eat and drink," He said, "for you are much more precious in God's sight than these birds. God will provide what you need."

293

Jesus went on to say, "And why do you worry about your clothes? Look at the lilies growing wild in the fields. They do not make their own clothing, yet they are dressed as splendidly as a king. Our God has provided clothing for flowers; don't you think He will provide clothing for you? Have faith! Do not worry."

God has given us a promise:
Serve God first and seek
to do the right things, and
He will give to you all
these other things.
That's a promise!

Affirmation: I will serve God first!

DO NOT JUDGE OTHERS   *Matthew 7:1-5*

God does not want us to judge another person's actions. That will be His job. Rather, He wants us to be concerned about our own actions. That's why Jesus said, "Do not judge others, or you too will be judged. And in the very same way you judge others, you will be judged."

Each of us has done things that were not pleasing to God. In God's eyes, we are all sinners. Jesus said, "Before you tell your neighbor about a speck of sawdust in his eye, first take the plank out of your own eye. Then you will see things more clearly."

Affirmation: I will not judge others!

ASK, SEEK, AND KNOCK

***Matthew 7:7** Ask and it will be given to you; seek and you will find; knock and the door will be opened to you*

Matthew writes concerning prayer, "Sometimes it takes a little time for prayers to be answered. But Jesus taught the people that they should never stop praying. Keep asking in prayer, and it will be given to you; keep seeking, and you will find what you are looking for; keep knocking, and the door will be opened for you! For God always hears our prayers. And He will answer; sometimes yes, sometimes no, sometimes wait."

"If you were a father and your child asked for bread, would you give him a stone? Or if your child asked for a fish, would you give him a snake? If we know how to give good gifts to our children, think of how much our Heavenly Father will give good gifts to those that ask Him! Treat others like you would want them to treat you: this is the golden rule!"

Affirmation: I will treat others like I would like them to treat me.

Ask, Seek, and Knock

Ask and it will be given to you; seek and you will find;
knock and the door will be opened to you.   (Matthew 7:7)

Verse: Ask and it will be giv-en to you, seek and you will find, knock and the door will be op - ened to you, for ev - 'ry - one who asks, re - ceives, yes, ev - 'ry - one who asks, re - ceives.

Chorus: Ask, seek, and knock. Ask, seek, and knock. For with these keys, I do believe, the treasures of heaven unlock. Just ask, seek, and knock. Ask, seek, and knock. Please understand by faith we can if we ask, seek, and knock.

THE WISE AND FOOLISH BUILDERS

Matthew 7:24 Everyone who hears these words of mine and puts them into practice is like a wise man who built his house upon the rock.

Jesus said that everyone who hears the word of God and does what it says is like a wise man who built his house upon a rock. Our "house" is our life and "the rock" is God's Word! When we build our lives on the solid rock of God's Word, we will stand! When the rains of trouble come, we will stand! When the streams of sickness rise, we will stand! When the winds of change come and beat against our house, it will not fall down! Because it is built on the solid rock of God's Word!

Now when Jesus finished His teaching, the crowd was amazed because He knew everything about the kingdom of God.

Affirmation: I will build my life on God's Word!

299

The Wise Man Built
His House Upon A Rock

*Everyone who hears these words of mine
and puts them into practice is like a wise man who
built his house upon the rock. (Matthew 7:24)*

Chorus: Now ev-ery-one who hears these words of mine to-day and puts them in-to prac-tice, prac-tice right a-way, is like a wise man who built his house up-on the rock and the rains came "tum-ba-ling" down.

Verse I: The wise man built his house upon the rock. The wise man built his house upon the rock. The wise man built his house upon the rock and the rains came "tumbaling" down.

Verse II: The foolish man built his house upon the sand. The foolish man built his house upon the sand. The foolish man built his house upon the sand and the rains came "tumbaling" down.

Verse III: So build your house on the Lord Jesus Christ. So build your house on the Lord Jesus Christ. So build your house on the Lord Jesus Christ and the blessings will come down.

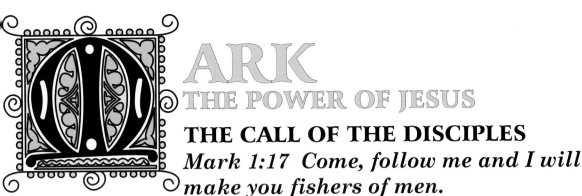

MARK
THE POWER OF JESUS

THE CALL OF THE DISCIPLES
Mark 1:17 Come, follow me and I will make you fishers of men.

Mark was a friend of Peter's who wrote down some of the stories Peter told about Jesus. One day as Jesus was walking beside the Sea of Galilee, He saw Peter and Peter's brother, Andrew. They were fishermen. "Come follow Me," Jesus said, "and I will make you fishers of men." At once they left their fishing nets and followed Him.

When they had gone a little further, they met James and his brother John who were also fishermen. As they were fixing their nets, Jesus said, "Come follow Me."

Without delay, they left their boat and followed Jesus.

Sometime later, Jesus had called twelve men to be his disciples. They would spend time with him and learn God's Word. Then someday they would go out and preach the good news! They were Peter, Andrew, James, John, Philip, Bartholomew, Matthew, Thomas, another James, Thaddaeus, Simon, and Judas.

Simon

John

Thomas

James

Thaddaeus

Philip

Judas

Matthew

James Too!

Bartholomew

Andrew

Peter

Affirmation: I want to be a disciple of Jesus too!

Come Follow Me

Come, follow me and I will make you fishers of men.   *(Mark 1:17)*

Chorus: Come fol-low me, come fol-low me, come fol-low me dis-ci-ples. Come fol-low me, come fol-low me, I'll make you fish-ers of men.

Verse: Je-sus, He saw a sail-boat. Je-sus saw nets and oars. Je-sus, He need-ed help-ers, so He called out to those on board.

Verse II: Peter, I need a helper. James, won't you come here? John, I need a helper. We need to tell them the Lord is near.

Verse III: Now, they all followed Jesus. No more nets and oars. Now they were very happy, now they followed Christ, the Lord.

Verse IV: Peter is now a helper. John, a helper, too. James is now a helper. He still needs more like me and you.

303

JESUS HEALS PETER'S MOTHER-IN-LAW

Mark 1:29-31

One day Peter came to Jesus and told Him about his mother-in-law who was very sick. Mark writes: "Together they went to her bed where she lay with a terrible fever. Jesus reached out and gently took her by the hand. With His touch, the fever suddenly left her. She was healed by the miracle touch of Jesus!"

Affirmation: I will call upon the Lord to heal me!

ROOFTOP MIRACLE   *Mark 2:1-12*

One day, Jesus was teaching in a home in Capernaum. The crowd grew so big that there was no room to stand inside. Even the doorways were jammed with people.

Some men came to see Jesus that day. They brought their friend who was sick and could not move. They believed that Jesus would heal him. "This crowd is too big," they said. "How will our friend ever see Jesus?" Then they had an idea!

The four men carried their friend, who lay on a mat, up to the roof. They began tearing away the rooftop to make a large hole right above Jesus! Then they lowered their friend down through the hole and he came to rest right in front of the Lord. Jesus knew these men must have great faith to do such a thing. So He said to the sick man, "Your sins are forgiven. Get up, take your mat, and go home."

Suddenly the man felt strength coming back into his arms and legs. He raised up ... he could move! Then he leaped off the mat and walked right through the crowd praising God!

Jesus had taken away his sickness and his sin, all in one miracle moment! This amazed everyone and they praised God, giving thanks saying, "We have never seen anything like this."

Affirmation: I will lead my friends to Jesus.

JESUS CALMS THE STORM   *Mark 4:35-41*

Mark tells us of another miracle Jesus did. "On another day,
Jesus was teaching the people by a lake. Once again the
crowds grew so big that Jesus had to get into a boat and
float away from the shore. Then everyone could hear
Him. There He sat and taught the people
many lessons of faith."

When evening came, Jesus was very tired. "Let's go over to the other side of the lake," He said. So they left the crowds behind and set sail across the lake. Jesus went to sleep on a cushion in the back of the sailboat. Suddenly, a terrible storm came up. The waves began to break over the sides of the boat, tossing it back and forth.

The disciples were frightened. They thought they might die, so they turned to Jesus. "Teacher!" they shouted. "Don't You care if we drown? Help us!" Jesus got up, faced the wind and the waves and shouted, "Quiet! Be still!" And at His word, the wind stopped blowing and the waters were calm.

Then Jesus said to His disciples, "Why were you so frightened? Where is your faith?" The disciples thought, "Who is this man? Even the wind and waves obey Him!"

Affirmation: I will run to Jesus when I am afraid.

FIVE LOAVES AND TWO FISH

Mark 6:41 Looking up to heaven, he gave thanks!

The news of Jesus' miracles began to
spread all over the land. People came to Jesus
from everywhere bringing Him their hurts
and sickness; and Jesus loved them ... every one!

But now He needed some rest. "Let us go to a quiet place,"
said Jesus. So they set sail across the lake. As they sailed
away, the people ran around the lake and were waiting for
them when they reached the other side.

When Jesus saw them, He loved them. They were like sheep without a shepherd; and after all, He was the Great Shepherd! So once again, He began teaching them and taking care of them.

It was late when the disciples said, "Jesus, send the people away so they can eat." But to their surprise He said, "You feed them."

"Feed them!" exclaimed the disciples. "That would cost too much!" Then Andrew spoke up. "There is a boy here with five loaves of bread and two fish. But how far will that go among so many?"

Then Jesus said to tell the people to sit down on the grass. As they were sitting down, Jesus took the five loaves and two fish and looked up into heaven. He thanked God and then began to break the loaves and fish into pieces.

Five thousand people were fed that day, and they all left with their bellies full. The disciples picked up twelve baskets full of bread and fish left behind by the crowd. Jesus has the power to supply all of our needs, no matter what!

Affirmation: Jesus will supply all my needs!

Loaves and Fishes

Looking up to heaven, he gave thanks! (Mark 6:41)

Verse I: Then Je - sus took the five lit - tle loaves,

Then Je - sus took the two lit - tle fish,

Then look - ing up to heav - en He

gave thanks, He gave thanks.

Look - ing up to heav - en, He gave thanks.

Verse II: Five thousand were fed with five little loaves. Five thousand were fed with two little fish. Then looking up to heaven, He gave thanks, He gave thanks. Looking up to heaven, He gave thanks.

315

FOOTPRINTS ON THE WATER

Mark 6:50 Take courage! It is I. Don't be afraid.

Jesus asked the disciples to sail ahead to Bethsaida while He said goodbye to the crowds. After they had gone, He went into the hills alone to pray.

When evening came, a mighty wind blew across the lake. The disciples could hardly row. Mark writes, "Jesus saw their trouble and went out to them, walking on the water!"

When they saw something coming toward them, they thought it was a ghost. They were very frightened! Then Jesus shouted, "It is I ... don't be afraid!" Peter said, "Lord, if it's You, tell me to come to You on the water." Jesus commanded, "Come."

Peter stepped out of the boat and walked to Jesus. But the mighty wind and the waves caused him to be afraid and lose faith. Then he began to sink.
"Lord save me!"
cried Peter.

Jesus reached out His hand and caught Peter. "Why did you doubt?" asked Jesus. Then they both climbed into the boat.

All the men worshiped Jesus saying, "Truly You are the Son of God!"

Affirmation: I will trust Jesus for a miracle!

Footprints On The Water

Take courage! It is I. Don't be afraid. (Mark 6:50)

When I was a lit-tle fish, swim-ming hap-pi-ly, I

heard the sound of foot-steps walk-ing on the sea. I

swam up to the sur-face and much to my sur-prise,

there on top of the wat-er, right be-fore my eyes, And I saw

foot-prints on the wat-er, foot-prints on the sea,

foot-prints on the wat-er, and I could not be-lieve, I saw

Je-sus, Je-sus walk-ing on the waves,

foot-prints on the wa-ter that day.

Verse II: Then a man, named Peter, stepped out on the waves. He tried to walk to Jesus; then, he sank away. This is how it happened; I heard Jesus say, "Take courage! It is I so don't be afraid."

LUKE
THE PARABLES OF JESUS
THE PARABLE OF THE SOWER
Luke 8

Once while a large crowd was gathering to see Jesus, He told this parable: "A farmer went out to plant his seeds. He took a handful and tossed them onto the ground."

"Some landed on the pathway to be stepped on and eaten by birds. Some landed upon the rocks, but before they could grow strong, they withered because their roots had no rich earth beneath them.

Other seeds fell among the thorns and were choked as they began to grow. But some of the seeds fell into the moist, rich earth and they grew healthy and strong. At harvest time, there were many crops; a hundred times more than the farmer sowed."

Then Jesus explained the meaning of the parable. "The seed is the Word of God. And like the seeds that fell along the pathway, some people hear the Word and receive it, but then the devil comes and confuses them and they no longer pay attention to God's Word. Because of this, they cannot be saved. And like the seeds that fell on the rocks, some people hear the Word of God and receive it with great joy. But then, when a time of trouble comes, they quickly fall away. This is because they have no deep roots of faith."

"The seeds that fall into the thorns are people who hear the Word of God and want to receive it, but their worries and cares of this life choke it out and they do not grow in faith.

But some seeds fall into good soil and bear much fruit in God's kingdom. These are people who hear the Word of God. They memorize it, and work very hard to produce a good crop for the Lord."

Affirmation: I will bear much fruit in God's kingdom!

THE GOOD SAMARITAN   *Luke 10:27-37*

Once a lawyer asked Jesus this tricky question, "If we are to love our neighbor as ourselves, who then is our neighbor?" Jesus answered, "A man was traveling from Jerusalem to Jericho when he was attacked by robbers. They took everything he had. They beat him up and left him by the roadside nearly dead. Soon, a priest came along. But when he saw the man, he passed by on the other side of the road.

Another church worker came along. But seeing the man, he too, passed him by without helping him. But then came a Samaritan. He was from another country. But when he saw the man hurt and bleeding, he stopped and helped him. He bandaged his wounds, put him on his own donkey and took him to an inn. There he cared for the man.

The next day, he took two silver coins and gave them to the innkeeper. The Samaritan said, 'Take care of this man and if you spend more than this, I will repay you.'"

Then Jesus said to the lawyer, "Which one of the three men was a good neighbor?" The lawyer answered, "Why, the one who helped him!" "Go and do likewise," Jesus told him.

Affirmation: I will be a good neighbor!

THE MUSTARD SEED

Luke 17:6 (Matthew 17:20) If you have faith as a mustard seed, you (can) say to this mountain, Move ... and it (would) move.

Jesus once explained what the kingdom of God was like. Luke records Jesus' words. Jesus said, "The kingdom of God is like a tiny little mustard seed which a farmer planted in his garden. When it received the rain and rich soil, it grew and became a great tree; strong enough for birds to sit in its branches."

The kingdom of God is in our hearts. It starts with just a little love and just a little faith. But then, as God helps us, we grow stronger and taller as believers!

Affirmation: I will grow stronger and taller as a believer!

Mustard Seed Faith

If you have faith as a mustard seed, you (can) say to this
mountain, Move ... and it (would) move.
Luke 17:6 (Matthew 17:20)

If you have faith   small as a must-ard seed,

If you have faith   small as a must-ard seed,

You   can   say   to   this   moun - tain,

move from here to there.   If   you have faith

small as a must-ard seed.   Noth-ing, noth-ing,

noth - ing will be   im - pos - si - ble!

Noth-ing, noth-ing will   be im-pos-si-ble. Oh,

ONE LOST SHEEP   *Luke 15:1-7*

The church leaders in Jesus' day began to say bad things about Him because He invited tax collectors and sinners to eat with him. So Jesus told this parable to show them that God loves everyone.

"What if you had a hundred sheep and one was lost? Wouldn't you leave the ninety-nine sheep in the meadow and look until you found the lost one?"

"And when you found him, wouldn't you be happy and carry the little lamb home on your shoulders? Then you'd call your friends together and say, 'Come celebrate with me for I have found my lost sheep!'

In the very same way, there is more celebration in heaven when one sinner comes to the Lord than over ninety-nine who do not need to repent. God is looking for lost sinners."

Affirmation: I will seek the lost!

THE PRODIGAL SON *Luke 15:11-32*

Jesus told this parable to His disciples. There once lived a man who had two sons. One day, the younger son came to his father and said, "Father, I would like my share of your property now." For he was to receive half when his father died. His father gave him his share.

The son then took the money and all that he owned and traveled to a far away country. There, he spent all his money having a good time and doing things his father had taught him not to do.

Then a terrible famine swept across the country and the boy had no money for food. He was very hungry!

To stay alive he took a job feeding pigs. He got so hungry, he would have eaten the pig food if someone had offered it to him. "My father's workers have plenty to eat," he thought. "I'll go back home and say, 'Father, I have disobeyed God and I have disobeyed you. I am not worthy to be called your son. But please, I only ask that you make me one of your workers.'" He left for home with a broken heart.

While the boy was still far from the house, his father saw him coming. His heart was filled with love and mercy. He ran as fast as he could. "My son ... my son has come home!" he shouted.

He threw his arms around the boy and kissed him. "Father, I have disobeyed God and I have disobeyed you. I am no longer worthy to be called your son," said the boy.

But his father replied, "Quickly, bring me our finest robe and put it on my son. Put a ring on his finger and new shoes on his feet. Let us prepare the biggest meal ever and celebrate. For my son who I thought was dead is alive; he was lost, but now is found!"

Meanwhile, the older brother had come in from working in the fields. When he heard the music and dancing he asked, "What's all this celebration?"

A servant replied, "Your brother has come home and your father is preparing a big meal!" This angered the older brother, and he refused to go into the house.

His father came outside and pleaded with him, but his son answered, "For years I have worked for you and done everything you have asked. Yet you never honored me in any way or celebrated my loyalty. But when this son of yours comes home after wasting all that you gave him, you have a celebration. It's not fair!"

"My son," said his father, "you are always with me. I love you and think of you always. Everything that I have is yours. But we must celebrate the homecoming of your brother ... for the son I thought to be dead is alive; he was lost, but now is found!"

This parable taught us that it is never too late to come back to God, for He always loves you!

Affirmation: I will be glad when sinners come to Jesus!

JOHN THE PROMISES OF JESUS

The book of John was written by one of Jesus' disciples, John. John tells us, "In the very beginning when God was creating the heavens and the earth, Jesus was there with Him. Together, they created Adam and Eve, all the birds and animals, and this world we live in."

"Then 2,000 years ago, this same Jesus came into our world as a baby and grew to be the God/man who died for our sins." Jesus gives some wonderful promises to live by in the book of John.

HE PROMISES TO LOVE US   *John 14:21*

John writes; Jesus taught His followers many lessons about love. We are to love our neighbor as ourself. We are to love God and Jesus promises to love us! He said, "Anyone who loves Me will be loved by My Heavenly Father and I will show them love too!" How do we show Jesus we love Him? Jesus said, "If anyone loves Me, they will obey My teachings."

Affirmation: I will obey Jesus!

HE PROMISES TO GUIDE US   *John 14:6*

One day Thomas, a disciple of Jesus, asked Him a very important question. "Lord, how can we know which way to go?" Jesus answered, "I am the Way and the Truth and the Life. No one comes to our Heavenly Father without first finding forgiveness in Me." If we follow the teachings of Jesus found in the Bible and pray, we will be on the right path!

Affirmation: I will follow Jesus!

HE PROMISES TO PROTECT US *John 10:11*

John writes; Jesus once said that we are like sheep and He was the Good Shepherd. Sheep do not know which way to go, so they listen for the Good Shepherd's voice and follow. Sheep never follow a stranger's voice; in fact, they run away from strangers. Jesus said, "I am the Good Shepherd, and the good shepherd is ready to die protecting His sheep." Jesus loves you and He will take care of you!

Affirmation: Jesus will take care of me!

343

HE PROMISES TO COMFORT US   *John 14:1-2*

Jesus said, "Do not let your hearts be troubled. Don't be filled with sorrow and sadness. Trust in God, for He is able to comfort you. Trust also in Me, for you have so much to look forward to! Keep your eyes fixed on heaven, for I'm going there to prepare a place just for you."

Affirmation: I will trust Jesus to comfort me!

HE PROMISES TO SEND THE HOLY SPIRIT
John 14:16-17

Jesus said that if we love Him, we will obey His commandments. He said, "I will ask My Heavenly Father, and He will send the Holy Spirit to those who love God. He will walk with you and guide you each and every day, and He will teach you all things and will remind you of everything I have said to you."

Affirmation: I will walk with the Holy Spirit!

HE PROMISES TO ANSWER PRAYER
John 16:23-24

Jesus taught His followers to pray. Prayer is talking to God. And since God is our dearest and closest friend, we should talk to Him every day.

Does God answer our prayers? Jesus said, "I tell you the truth, My Heavenly Father will give you whatever you ask for in prayer if you ask in My name." This means we should pray for things that would please Jesus.

Affirmation: I will pray for things that please Jesus!

HE PROMISES US ETERNAL LIFE

John 3:16 For God so loved the world, that He gave His only begotten Son.

How long do most people live? Some live to be 70 years old, some 80, a few even 100 years old. The greatest promise of all in the Bible is the one Jesus made in John 3:16.

"For God so loved the world (that means you and me) that He gave His only begotten Son (that's Jesus!) that whosoever believes in Him should not perish (that means they will never die), but have everlasting life." If we love God, someday we will live with Jesus in heaven forever!

Affirmation: I want to go to heaven!

347

For God So Loved The World

For God so loved the world, that He gave
His only begotten Son. (John 3:16)

Chorus: For God so loved the world,
God so loved the world, God so
loved the world, He gave His on-ly
Son, Son, Verse: That who-so-ev-er be-
liev-eth in Him, in Him
should not per-ish but have e-ter-nal
life. A - men.

348

JOURNEY to the CROSS
Luke 18-24

The feast of the Passover was only a few short days away. Jesus called His disciples together and said, "We are going to Jerusalem. There, all the things written about Me by the prophets will happen. I will be handed over to Roman leaders. I will be unkindly treated, and there I will die. But three days later I will come back to life again."

ZACCHAEUS

Luke 19:5 Zacchaeus,
come down immediately.
I must stay at your
house today.

On their way to Jerusalem,
Jesus and His disciples came
to the city of Jericho. It was
the home of a very rich man
named Zacchaeus. He was the chief
tax collector and not liked
by the people.

Zacchaeus wanted to see Jesus, but he was a very short man and could not see over the crowds. So he climbed up in a sycamore tree. From there he could see Jesus. When Jesus saw Zacchaeus, He said, "Come down, for I am going to stay at your house today." At once, Zacchaeus jumped down from the tree and welcomed Jesus into his home.

When the people saw Jesus being kind to Zacchaeus, they were very upset. They didn't know that Zacchaeus had changed! He said to Jesus, "I'm sorry for the way I have treated the people. I will pay back each one." Jesus was very happy and replied, "Today you are saved, and that is why I have come ... to save the lost!"

Affirmation: I want to see Jesus!

Zacchaeus

Zacchaeus, come down immediately.
I must stay at your house today. (Luke 19:5)

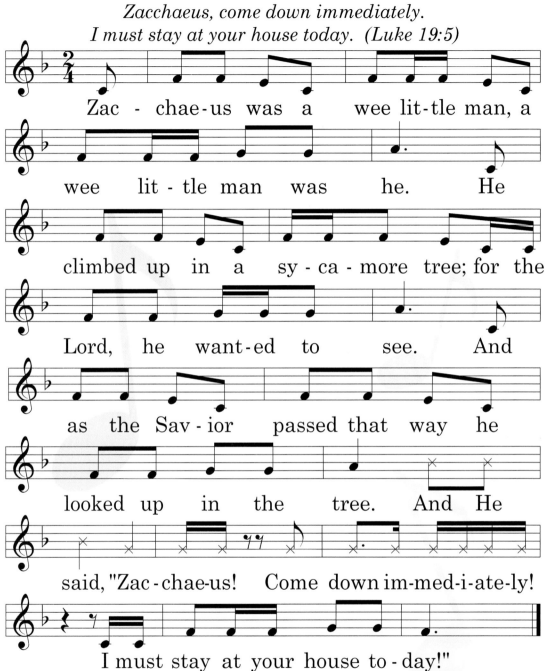

Zac - chae-us was a   wee lit-tle man, a

wee   lit - tle man   was   he.   He

climbed up in a   sy - ca - more tree; for the

Lord,   he   want-ed   to   see.   And

as   the Sav - ior   passed that way   he

looked up   in   the   tree.   And He

said, "Zac-chae-us!   Come down im-med-i-ate-ly!

I must stay at your house to - day!"

THE TRIUMPHAL ENTRY
Luke 19

On Sunday, Jesus came to the Mount of Olives, which is near Jerusalem. He sent two disciples ahead and told them, "As you enter the village, you will find a donkey which no one has ever ridden. Untie it and bring it to Me. If anyone asks what you are doing, say 'The Lord needs it.'"

The disciples obeyed Jesus and brought the donkey to Him.

They spread their coats over the donkey and put Jesus on his back. As Jesus approached Jerusalem, a huge crowd lined the road. Many spread their coats across the road and waved palm branches as if to welcome a hero! Together they shouted, "Hosanna to the King. Blessed is He who comes in the name of the Lord!"

Affirmation: I will bless the name of Jesus!

Blessed Is He

Blessed, Blessed is He, Blessed,

Blessed, Blessed is He, that

com-eth in the name of the Lord.

His name is Won-der-ful, Coun - se - lor,

Al - might-y God. He is the

Ev - er-last - ing Fath - er, He's the

Prince of Peace.

A HOUSE OF PRAYER *Luke 19*

On Monday, Jesus entered the temple in Jerusalem.   He
became very angry at the money changers and those buying
and selling doves in God's house. He overturned their
tables and drove them all out of the temple . Then He began
to teach, "Is it not written, 'My house shall be called a house
of prayer?' You have made it a robber's house!" When the
priests heard what Jesus had done, they wanted rid of Him.

On Tuesday, Jesus awoke and returned to Jerusalem. Once again, He was greeted by huge crowds who followed Him everywhere. The religious leaders began to worry. "What if Jesus leads the people against us? We could lose our power. We must stop Him!"

They said, "Let's trick Jesus into saying something bad about Rome. Then Rome will arrest Him, and we'll be done with Him!"

Affirmation: I will follow Jesus too!

THIRTY PIECES OF SILVER *Luke 22, Matthew 26*

That night Judas Iscariot, one of the twelve disciples, went in to see these church leaders. "I know that you want Jesus removed," he said. "What will you give me if I help you?" They counted out thirty pieces of silver. Judas agreed and started planning to betray Jesus.

Affirmation: *I will be faithful to Jesus!*

THE UPPER ROOM *Luke 22*

On Thursday evening, Jesus and His twelve disciples met in an upper room to celebrate the Passover. The meal was prepared by Peter and John. He taught them many things that evening. He said that being "the greatest" meant that we must serve others. Then He washed their feet as an example of what a servant does. When it came time to eat, Jesus took some bread, blessed it and gave it to His disciples saying, "Take this bread and eat it; for it is My body." And they all ate.

Then taking the cup, He gave thanks and said, "This is My blood, which is spilled out for many. Do this in remembrance of Me." And they all drank. This was the first communion service.

As the mealtime ended, Jesus spoke once more. "Tonight, I am giving you a new commandment. Love one another. If you do this, everyone will know you are My disciples." They sang a song and together they went back to the Mount of Olives.

PRAYER IN THE GARDEN *Luke 22*

Now there was a beautiful garden near the Mount of Olives called Gethsemane. Jesus and His disciples went there late Thursday night. Jesus said to them, "Sit here while I go and pray." He took Peter, James, and John with Him.

"My heart is about to break with sorrow," Jesus told them. "Please stay awake and keep watch for Me." Then Jesus walked a little further and fell to the ground praying.

"Father, if it is possible, let these terrible things which are about to happen go away. Yet I am willing to do what You want, not what I want."

And Jesus prayed so very hard that the sweat on His forehead became drops of blood falling to the ground.

When He returned to His disciples, He found them all asleep. Jesus returned to pray a second and third time. But each time He found his disciples sleeping. Then Jesus knew the worst was about to happen. "Look," He said, "My betrayer is coming!"

Affirmation: I want to do God's will!

THE BETRAYER COMES   *Luke 22; Matthew 26*

Through the darkness and down the narrow pathway came a mob of people carrying torches and clubs. Following was a small group of Roman soldiers. Judas was leading the way. He had told the mob to grab the one he would kiss and to take Him away.

With the mob behind him, Judas stood face to face with Jesus. "Master," said Judas. Then he kissed Jesus. The mob grabbed Him.

Peter pulled out his sword. While trying to protect Jesus, he swung and cut off the ear of one of the chief priest's guards. "Put away the sword!" shouted Jesus. Then Jesus reached out, touched, and healed the servant's ear. There in the darkness the Roman soldiers and the Jewish leaders bound Jesus and took Him away. The disciples were afraid and fled into the night.

Affirmation: With Jesus I am not afraid!

THE TRIALS OF JESUS
Luke 22-23; Matthew 27

Early Friday morning the many trials of Jesus began. People lied to judges about things Jesus had said and done. He was spat upon, beaten, and terribly abused.

When Judas saw what was happening to Jesus, he was filled with sorrow. He knew he had sinned. He went to the temple and begged them to release Jesus, but they would not listen. Judas threw his coins on the temple floor and ran away. He could no longer live with himself knowing what he had done to Jesus.

Finally, Jesus was brought before Pontius Pilate, the Roman governor and judge. The Jewish leaders kept saying things that were untrue. "He says that He is a king. And He says we should not pay taxes to Caesar!" Pilate looked at Jesus, who had been badly beaten, and asked, "Are You the King of the Jews?" Jesus replied, "My kingdom is not in this world."

"Then You are a king?" asked Pilate again. "You say correctly that I am a king," answered Jesus. "But I come to this world to tell people the truth."

"What is truth?" asked Pilate. Then he said, "I find no wrong in this man. Let him go."

Each year during the Passover celebration the Roman
governor would release one prisoner. The people would
decide which one. Pilate knew that the Jewish leaders were
accusing Jesus because they were jealous of Him. "The
people love Jesus," he thought. "So I'll let them choose
between Jesus and that terrible murderer named Barabbas.
Surely the people will choose Jesus!"

So Pilate spoke to the crowd that had gathered. "Should Jesus be set free, or Barabbas?" To Pilate's surprise, he heard them shouting "Barabbas! Free Barabbas!"

"What shall I do with Jesus?" Pilate asked the crowd. "Kill Him! Crucify Him!" they shouted. Louder and louder their cries rang out until Pilate, fearing a riot, decided to please them.

Affirmation: I will choose Jesus to be my savior!

THE CRUCIFIXION
Luke 24:6 He has risen!

Jesus was then turned over to the Roman soldiers. They stripped off His clothes and beat Him with a whip. They made fun of Him by putting a purple robe on His back and placing a crown of thorns on His head.

Jesus was silent. Then they put His own clothes back on Him and led Him away to a place called Golgotha to be crucified.

On Friday morning they crucified Jesus and two lawbreakers, one on the right and the other on the left. As Jesus hung on the cross He was heard to say, "Father forgive them, for they do not know what they are doing."

Then one of the lawbreakers hanging with Jesus said, "If you really are the King of the Jews, save Yourself!" But the other lawbreaker said, "Be quiet! We deserve to die because we have done many bad things. This man has done nothing wrong. Jesus, remember me."

Jesus looked at this man and said, "Today you will be with Me in heaven." A great darkness fell over the land for three hours. Jesus cried out from the cross with a loud voice, "It is finished! Father, I give to You My Spirit." And having said this, He died.

Jesus' body was placed in the borrowed tomb of a secret disciple named Joseph. They rolled a large stone in front of the opening and went away.

On Sunday morning, a woman named Mary Magdalene and the other Mary came to the tomb. They found the giant stone had been rolled away. Upon the stone sat an angel who said, "Jesus is not here. He is alive! Quickly now, go tell His disciples."

They ran like the wind to tell the disciples. "Jesus has risen! He's alive!" They were so happy!

Jesus appeared to many people. He walked with two followers on the Emmaus Road. Then Jesus visited the disciples in Jerusalem as they gathered to eat supper. "Peace be with you," Jesus said. He ate with them and showed them His nail-scarred hands and feet.

Jesus was truly alive ... He had risen from the grave! "Remember what I said on the way to Jerusalem several days ago? 'I will be handed over to the Roman leaders. I will be unkindly treated and, just like the prophets said, I will die and on the third day I will come back to life again.' All these things you have now seen."

"Now you must go into every nation and tell them the good news of God's coming kingdom. Tell them that if they believe in Me and My words, they will live forever, just like Me!"

Jesus stayed with the disciples a while longer. Then after He had blessed each of them, He said, "I am going now to live with My Father and your Father. Be sure that I am always going to be with you."

Then Jesus rose up into the air until He disappeared in the clouds.

As they were gazing into the sky, two men in white clothing stood beside them and said, "One day Jesus will come again in this very same way." Then the disciples returned to Jerusalem to start their ministries.

Affirmation: I believe Jesus died and rose again for me!

He Has Risen

He has risen! (Luke 24:6)

Verse III: He has ris - en, this we sing,

Lord and Mas - ter, King of kings.

He has ris - en to for - give.

Tell the world that Je - sus lives.

Chorus: Yes, Je - sus loves me! Yes, Je - sus

loves me! Yes, Je - sus loves me! The

Bi - ble tells me so!

Verse I: Jesus loves me, this I know. For the Bible tells me so.
Little ones to Him belong; they are weak but He is strong.
Verse II: Jesus loves me, He will stay, close beside me all the
way. He's prepared a home for me, and some day His face I'll see.

ACTS

BLINDED BY THE LIGHT

Acts 2:21 Everyone who calls on the name of the Lord shall be saved.

Many of the Jewish religious leaders continued to treat the Christian believers in a very unkind way. Saul of Tarsus was probably the most unkind. He did not believe in the Lord Jesus. He had men and women who loved the Lord put in chains and taken away to terrible prisons.

One day as Saul and his friends were traveling to a city called Damascus, a very bright light suddenly shone around him. Then Saul heard a voice from heaven saying, "Saul, why are you so unkind to Me?" When Saul asked, "Who are You, Lord?" He heard the voice reply, "I am Jesus." Then Saul knew that Jesus really was alive!

The light was so brilliant that it blinded Saul. Trembling with fear Saul asked, "Lord, what do you want me to do?"

The Lord commanded him to go to Damascus, and Saul obeyed.

Three dark days later, God sent a good man named
Ananias to visit Saul. Suddenly, he could see again!
Saul praised God as Ananias told him about God's
special plan for his life. Later, Saul even changed
his name from Saul to Paul, for now he would
live for Jesus.

Affirmation: I will live for Jesus!

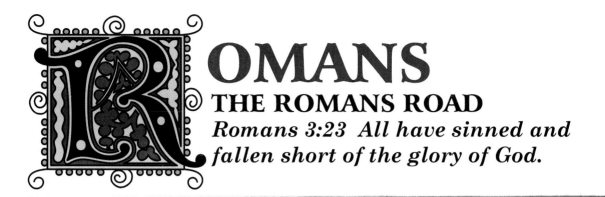

ROMANS

THE ROMANS ROAD

Romans 3:23 All have sinned and fallen short of the glory of God.

Paul was a letter writer. He wrote very special letters to the Christian churches of his time. Some of Paul's letters are in our Holy Bible ... like his letter to the Romans. In this letter, he tells us we can be saved by following these steps:

Romans 3:23 -For everyone has sinned and fallen short of the glory of God.
Romans 6:23 -For the wages of sin is death, but the gift of God is eternal life through Jesus Christ our Lord.
Romans 5:8 -But God showed His love for us in this way: while we were still sinners, Christ died for us.
Romans 10:10 -For it is with your heart that you believe and with your mouth that you confess and are saved.
Romans 10:13 -For everyone who calls on the name of the Lord will be saved.

Paul's wonderful letter to the Romans shows us how to lead a friend to Jesus.

Affirmation: I will lead a friend to Jesus!

378

All Have Sinned

All have sinned and fallen short of the glory of God.
(Romans 3:23)

All have sinned and fall - en short

of the glor - y of the Lord.

All have sinned, oh yes it's true.

Je - sus saved me, He'll save you. Hur -

ray! We're saved. Hur - ray! We're saved.

First CORINTHIANS

GOD'S KIND OF LOVE

1 Corinthians 13:4 Love is patient, love is kind.

There was a brand new group of Christians who started a church in the great city of Corinth, Greece. Corinth was full of idol worshipers and Paul had journeyed there many times to preach the good news of Jesus Christ. In one of his letters written to this growing church, he explained the meaning of "God's kind of Love." He wrote: "If I could speak with the words of an angel, but had no love inside my heart, I would only be making noise like a clanging cymbal.

If I knew all there was to know and could move mountains with my faith, I would still have an empty heart without love. If I gave everything I own to the poor, I would gain nothing if it wasn't given in love. When we have God's kind of love in our hearts, we are willing to be patient with others. When we have God's kind of love in our hearts, we don't become jealous of others, wanting what they may have.

When we have God's kind of love in our hearts, we never hurt anyone's feelings by being rude, and we always forgive others. When we have God's love in our hearts, we think of others first, not ourselves. We stay away from bad things and seek to do good things. When we have God's kind of love inside, we protect the helpless, and hope for the good. God's kind of love keeps on loving no matter what happens. That's why God's love is the greatest gift we can give to others."

Affirmation: I will show God's kind of love!

Love Is Patient

Love is patient, love is kind.   (1 Corinthians 13:4)

Love is pa-tient. Love is pa-tient.

Love is kind. Love is kind. Re -

joic - ing in the truth, re -

joic - ing in the truth

all the time, all the time.

Second CORINTHIANS

YOKED TOGETHER

2 Corinthians 6:14-15 Do not be yoked together with unbelievers ... what harmony is there between Christ and Belial (the devil)?

Several years after Paul had written his first letter to the Corinthians, the church began to have many problems. A missionary named Titus was sent by Paul to help the church grow. Titus was a great teacher and soon the people returned to God's way of doing things. When Titus returned with his good report, Paul was so excited!

Guided by the Holy Spirit, Paul wrote a second letter. His words tell us how to keep from falling into sin.

"Do not join a group of people who do not share your belief in Jesus. For what do good deeds and bad deeds have in common? What kind of friendship can light have with darkness? What do the teachings of Jesus and Satan have in common? What does a believer and an unbeliever have in common? Because you are a Christian, separate yourself from those who do bad things and God will be a Father to you and you will be His sons and daughters."

Affirmation: I want to have Christian friends!

Do Not Be Yoked

Do not be yoked together with unbelievers ... what harmony is there between Christ and Belial (the devil)? (2 Corinthians 6:14-15)

Do not be yoked to - geth - er with

un - be - liev - ing friends. Do

not be yoked to - geth - er with

un - be - liev - ing friends. Har - mon -

y, har-mon-y, what har-mon-y can there be be-

tween the Lord and the de - vil be - low? Oh

no, there's none you see.

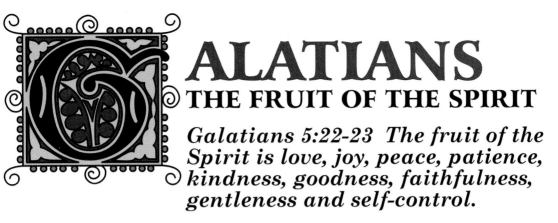

GALATIANS
THE FRUIT OF THE SPIRIT

Galatians 5:22-23 The fruit of the Spirit is love, joy, peace, patience, kindness, goodness, faithfulness, gentleness and self-control.

The missionary Paul wrote many letters to the early churches. He wrote this one to the church at Galatia. Like the Corinthians, they too were following false teachers who thought that good works alone made you a Christian. But we know that only faith in Jesus Christ makes us a Christian.

Paul's letter of love to the Galatians read as follows: People of Galatia, God does not measure us by the works of our hands. The only thing that matters is faith, and the love we give to others by faith.

387

So I say, let the Holy Spirit guide you and when He does, your life will bring forth fruit just like a fruit tree. But the fruit of the Spirit will be

LOVE
JOY
PEACE
PATIENCE
KINDNESS
GOODNESS
FAITHFULNESS
GENTLENESS
SELF-CONTROL

Let the Holy Spirit help you to be a fruitful person!

Affirmation: I will let the Holy Spirit guide me!

The Fruit Of The Spirit

The fruit of the Spirit is love, joy, peace, patience, kindness, goodness, faithfulness, gentleness and self-control. (Galatians 5:22-23)

Oh   the   fruit   of,   the

fruit of the Spir-it is, yes the fruit   of,   the

fruit of   the Spir - it   is   love   and

joy,   joy   and   peace,   peace   and

pa - tience   and kind - ness   too.   Gen - tle -

ness,   faith - ful - ness,   self - con -

trol   and   good - ness   for   you.   Cha - Cha - Cha!

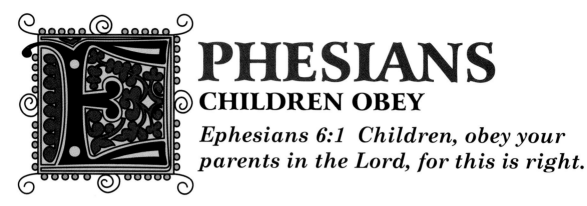

EPHESIANS
CHILDREN OBEY

Ephesians 6:1 Children, obey your parents in the Lord, for this is right.

Paul's letter to the church at Ephesus included some words just for children. Children, obey your parents in the Lord for this is right. Honor your father and mother which is the first commandment with a promise. God promises that things will be well with you and you will enjoy a long life on the earth.

Paul went on to explain that as followers of Jesus we are soldiers in the Lord's army. Satan is the enemy we fight.

So put on the whole armor of God. He gave these examples. Put on a **BELT OF TRUTH** and a **BREASTPLATE OF RIGHTEOUSNESS**. Cover your feet with the **GOSPEL OF PEACE**. Take up a **SHIELD OF FAITH** to protect you from Satan's fiery arrows. Put on the **HELMET OF SALVATION** and the **SWORD OF THE SPIRIT** which is the Bible. And pray about each decision and pray for your friends. Being a soldier isn't always fun, but God's army needs you every day to fight the good fight!

Affirmation: I am a soldier in the Lord's army!

Children, Obey Your Parents

Children, obey your parents in the Lord, for this is right.
(Ephesians 6:1)

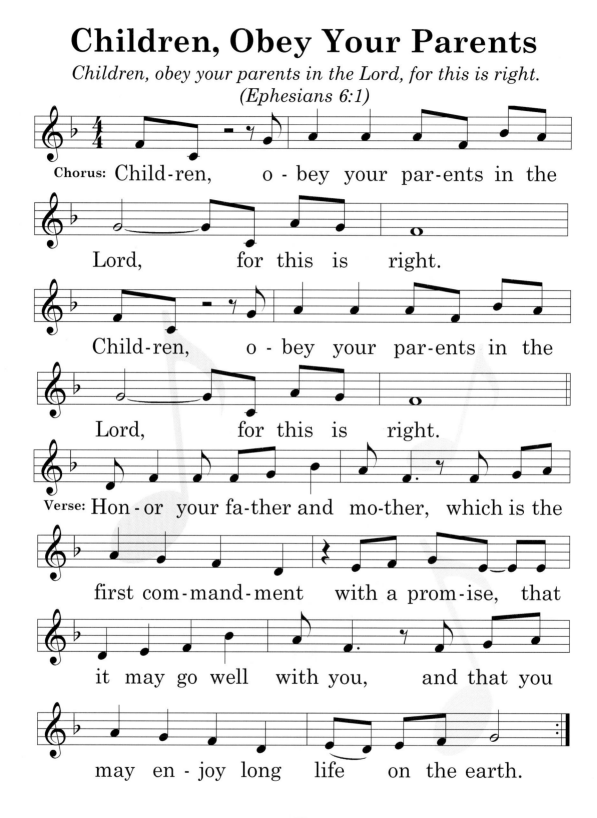

Chorus: Child-ren, o - bey your par-ents in the Lord, for this is right.

Child-ren, o - bey your par-ents in the Lord, for this is right.

Verse: Hon - or your fa-ther and mo-ther, which is the first com-mand-ment with a prom-ise, that it may go well with you, and that you may en - joy long life on the earth.

PHILIPPIANS
THINK ABOUT THESE THINGS

Philippians 4:8 Finally brothers, whatever is true, whatever is noble, whatever is right, whatever is pure, whatever is lovely, whatever is admirable,... think about such (these) things.

Once again Paul dips his pen into the ink and writes another letter. This time he addresses it to the believers in Philippi. "Thank you," he writes, "for all the many ways you have helped the cause of Christ. And be sure of this, that He who began a good work in you will help you to complete it. Our God is faithful. So continue to work without complaining or arguing and live together in peace. That way you will shine like stars in the universe."

"And finally brothers and sisters, whatever is true, whatever is noble, whatever is right, whatever is pure, whatever is lovely, whatever is admirable, think about these things. Practice what you preach and the God of peace will be with you. For this, friends, is the secret to being happy: we can do all things through Christ who strengthens us!"

Affirmation: I can do all things through Christ who strengthens me!

Think About These Things

Finally brothers, whatever is true, whatever is noble, whatever is right, whatever is pure, whatever is lovely, whatever is admirable,... think about such (these) things. (Philippians 4:8)

Oh, what should we think a-bout? Oh,

what should we think a-bout? Oh,

what should we think a-bout? Things so great,

found in Phil-lip-pi-ans 4: 8. Fin-ally broth-ers, what-

ev-er is true, what-ev-er is no-ble, what-

ev-er is right, What-ev-er is pure, what-

ev-er is love-ly, what-ev-er is ad-mir-able,

think a-bout such things.

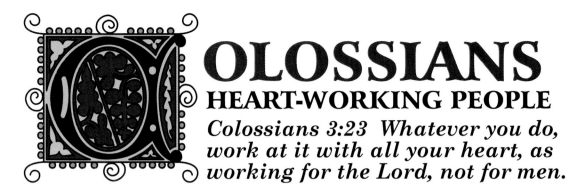

OLOSSIANS
HEART-WORKING PEOPLE

Colossians 3:23 Whatever you do, work at it with all your heart, as working for the Lord, not for men.

Paul taught the believers in the Colossian church that they had been rescued, much like a drowning man. Except we were rescued from the evil one and brought into God's kingdom. It's like being born again, for had we not been rescued and saved we would have died. Now we rejoice and we live for Jesus.

So whatever you do, work at it with all your heart as working for the Lord and not for men. For it is the Lord you are serving. Make the most of every opportunity God gives you. Do your very best!

Affirmation: I will do my very best at all times!

Working For The Lord

Whatever you do, work at it with all your heart, as working for the Lord, not for men. (Colossians 3:23)

When - ev-er we work, we'll do our best,

though the rest laugh and jest.

With the Lord, we'll stand the test and

al-ways do our best. What-

ev - er, what - ev - er you do,

work at it with all your heart, as

work - ing for the Lord and

not for men. When -

First HESSALONIANS

EVERY DAY IS PRAY DAY!

I Thessalonians 5:16-18 Be joyful always; pray without ceasing, in everything give thanks.

Paul had a great love and pleasant memories of the church in Thessalonica. Their faith and love of God had grown even while they were being treated very harshly. They shared the Word of God with others and they lived it every day. They believed, as we do, that Jesus is alive and someday He is coming back to this earth to claim us as His people. Because of this wonderful news, Paul writes, "Rejoice always, pray without ceasing, and in everything give thanks!"

Affirmation: I will rejoice and pray!

Be Joyful Always

Be joyful always; pray without ceasing, in everything
give thanks.   (1 Thessalonians 5:16-18)

Be joy - ful al - ways.   Pray with - out

ceas - ing.   Be joy - ful

al - ways.   Pray with - out

ceas - ing.   Be joy - ful

al - ways.   Pray with - out

ceas - ing;   no turn - ing

back,   no turn - ing back.

Verse I: I have decided to follow Jesus. (3 times) No turning back, no turning back.
Verse III: In everything, child, give thanks and praise Him. (3 times) No turning back, no turning back.

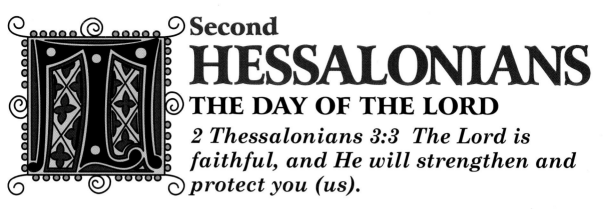

Second
HESSALONIANS
THE DAY OF THE LORD

2 Thessalonians 3:3 The Lord is faithful, and He will strengthen and protect you (us).

In Paul's second letter to the Thessalonians he warns the believer that false teachers would come into the church. He writes, "Beware! These teachers will be able to work certain kinds of miracles. But Satan is the source of their power. So pray for us that we may escape their evil traps. For we know the Lord is faithful, and He will strengthen and protect us from the evil one."

Affirmation: The Lord will strengthen and protect me!

The Lord Is Faithful

*The Lord is faithful, and He will strengthen and
protect you (us).   (2 Thessalonians 3:3)*

The   Lord   is faith - ful   and   He   will,

and   He   will,   and   He   will,   the

Lord   is   faith - ful   and   He   will

strength-en   and   pro - tect   us.   The

Lord   is   faith - ful   and   He   will,

and   He   will,   and   He   will,   the

Lord is faith-ful and He will guide and di-rect us.

Verse II: The Lord is faithful and He will, and He will, and He will,
the Lord is faithful and He will love and correct us.

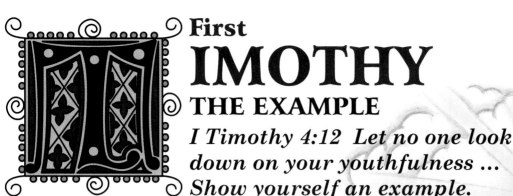

First IMOTHY
THE EXAMPLE

I Timothy 4:12 Let no one look down on your youthfulness ... Show yourself an example.

In a letter to his dear friend Timothy, Paul tells him to be about God's work, which is saving lost sinners. We are also to pray for the leaders of our country.

Then Paul writes some very important words, "For there is one God, and one peacemaker who stands between God and men; that man is Jesus Christ who gave Himself as a payment for our sin. This is the gospel message to young and old. Therefore, let no one look down on you because you are young; but rather set an example for those who believe."

Affirmation: I will set a good example!

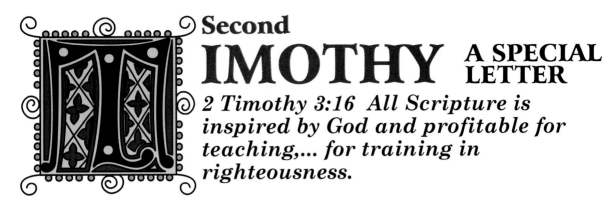

Second IMOTHY — A SPECIAL LETTER

2 Timothy 3:16 All Scripture is inspired by God and profitable for teaching,... for training in righteousness.

Paul wrote a second letter to his missionary friend Timothy. In it, God tells us that all scripture in our Holy Bible is given by inspiration of the Holy Spirit. It is profitable for teaching and for training people to live holy lives. These precious Bible verses make us spiritually ready to do the work of God. Some may preach the Word. Some may teach, but all must serve. The Bible says that a day is soon coming when many people will no longer believe in God. Let us therefore, work today, for the hour is late.

Affirmation: I will serve the Lord!

TITUS MERCY, MERCY ME

Titus 3:5 God saved us, not because of righteous things we had done, but because of his mercy.

Once a young pastor in the ancient city of Crete opened a letter sent to him by Paul. It was a very short, but powerful letter. It read, "Teach the people of Crete the truth of God's word. Teach the older men to be self-controlled and to love one another. Teach the older women to live in a loving and kind way, never harming others with unkind or untrue words." Jesus wanted them to set an example for younger Christians.

And always remember, God saved us not because of righteous things we had done, but because of His mercy. So please learn to do what is good in His sight.

Grace be with you!

Affirmation: I will do what is good!

God Saved Us

God saved us, not because of righteous things we had done, but because of his mercy.   (Titus 3:5)

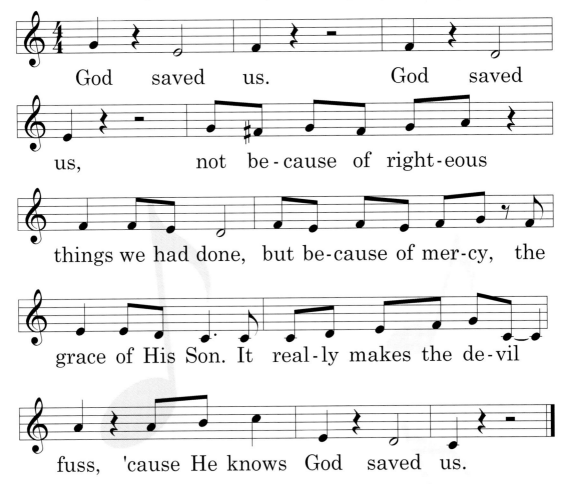

God   saved   us.   God   saved

us,   not be‑cause of   right‑eous

things we had done,   but be‑cause of mer‑cy,   the

grace of His Son. It   real‑ly makes the de‑vil

fuss,   'cause He knows God   saved   us.

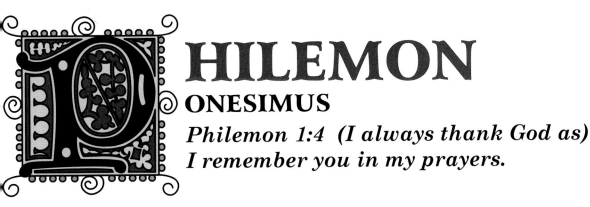

PHILEMON
ONESIMUS

Philemon 1:4 (I always thank God as)
I remember you in my prayers.

Paul was arrested for preaching the gospel while in the city of Rome. This letter was written from his prison cell to a wealthy friend named Philemon. Philemon had a slave named Onesimus who had stolen from him and run away to Rome to hide. But while there, Onesimus met Paul and gave his heart to Jesus. He then decided to return to his master to make things right again.

407

So Paul writes, "I thank God always, making mention of you in my prayers." Then he explained that Onesimus was no longer a slave, but a brother in Christ. He asked Philemon to welcome Onesimus home as he would welcome Paul himself. "If he has done you any wrong," Paul writes, "or if he owes you any money, charge it to me and I will pay it back." Paul loved Onesimus and prayed for his safe return.

Affirmation:
I will pray
for my friends!

408

Kum Ba Ya

(I always thank God as) I remember you in my prayers. (Philemon 1:4)

Verse I: I re - mem - ber you in my prayers. I re - mem - ber you in my prayers. I re - mem - ber you in my prayers. Thank - ing God in my prayers.

Verse II: Someone's praying Lord, Kum ba ya. Someone's praying Lord, Kum ba ya. Someone's praying Lord, Kum ba ya. Oh, Lord, Kum ba ya.

Verse III: Someone's crying Lord, Kum ba ya. Someone's crying Lord, Kum ba ya. Someone's crying Lord, Kum ba ya. Oh, Lord, Kum ba ya.

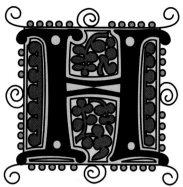

HEBREWS THE HALL OF FAITH

Hebrews 11:6 For without faith, it is impossible to please God.

What does faith mean? It is believing what God says in his Word and acting on it. "For without faith, it is impossible to please God."

The book of Hebrews presents a list of ordinary men and women who became heroes of faith.

Let's take a tour of God's Hall of Faith found in the book of Hebrews.

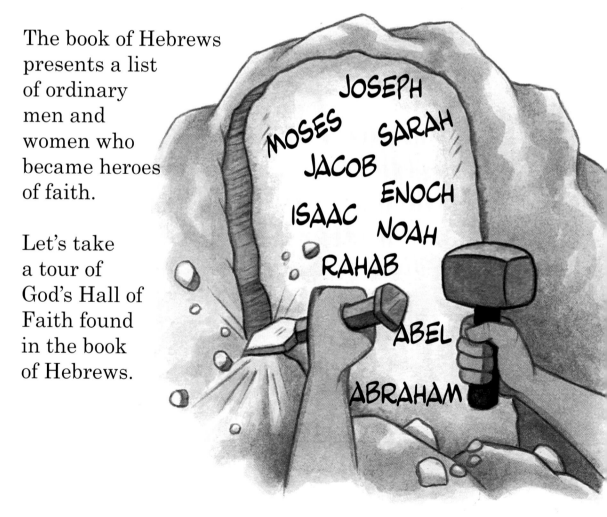

JOSEPH
MOSES   SARAH
JACOB
ENOCH
ISAAC   NOAH
RAHAB
ABEL
ABRAHAM

ABEL: By faith Abel offered God a blood sacrifice which pleased Him.

NOAH: By faith Noah obeyed God, building an ark miles from any sea.

ABRAHAM: By faith Abraham left his home for a place God would show him.

SARAH: By faith Sarah believed God's promise and had a baby at age 90.

ISAAC: By faith Isaac passed the promises of God on to his sons.

ABRAHAM

JOSEPH

SARAH

NOAH

JACOB: By faith Jacob, as he was dying, blessed the sons of Joseph.

JOSEPH: By faith Joseph commanded his bones be taken to Canaan where God would fulfill His promise.

MOSES: By faith Moses believed God, choosing to suffer with the people of God.

RAHAB: By faith Rahab believed that Israel's God was true and hid the spies.

JACOB

ISAAC

My picture here

RAHAB

MOSES

_____
My name

Affirmation: My faith is going to grow!

Have Faith

For without faith, it is impossible to please God. (Hebrews 11:6)

Chorus: Have faith, have faith. Peo - ple now,

have faith, have faith. Peo - ple now,

have faith, have faith, trust - ing in

Je - sus, be-lieve us. For

with-out faith it's im - pos - si - ble

to please God, so live a life that's full and

have faith, have faith; God 'll see you through.

Verse: There's a book in the Bible; Hebrews is the place. Listed there are the heroes, the heros of our faith. Abel and Enoch and Rahab, too, (2nd time - Abraham, Isaac, Jacob, too,) walked by faith; so can you. Just have faith, have faith; God'll see you through.

413

JAMES THE LORD'S BROTHER

James 1:19 But let everyone be quick to hear (listen), slow to speak, and slow to become angry.

The book of James was written by Jesus' brother, James. At first, James did not believe in Jesus. But after Jesus rose from the dead, he believed and wrote this wonderful book on faith. "Take note," he writes, "everyone should be quick to listen, slow to speak, and slow to become angry. But do not listen only; do what God's Word says!

And remember, your tongue is like the rudder on a large sailing ship. Even though a ship is large and driven by strong winds, it is steered by a very small rudder. In the very same way, our tongues are small, but they can make big boasts.

Out of the same mouth we can praise God and say bad things. This should not be. Can fresh water and salt water flow from the same spring? Neither should our tongues praise and say bad things."

Affirmation: I will only say good things!

Be Quick To Listen

But let everyone be quick to hear (listen), slow
to speak, and slow to become angry. (James 1:19)

Bet - ter   to   be slow.

Bet-ter to be slow   for a   quick tem-pered man does

fool - ish things. Bet - ter   to be slow.

Bet - ter   to be slow.   If you've got - ta be quick, be

quick   to lis - ten,   slow   to speak and

slow to be - come an - gry.   So be quick, be

quick to lis - ten   and be slow to   speak

First PETER

THE HUMBLE NEVER CRUMBLE

I Peter 5:6 Humble yourselves (therefore) under God's mighty hand.

Peter addressed his wonderful letter to God's chosen people. He calls us "strangers in this world." Now strangers are people who have a home somewhere else. They're just visiting for a while. Peter knew that a Christian's true home is in heaven. We live here as "strangers," seeking first the things of God, not the things of gold and glory. This is very strange indeed to worldly people.

GOLD GOD

But Peter says, "Humble yourselves under God's mighty hand. This means we should set aside our own wants and wishes and do the things that please God. Be self-controlled; for our enemy, Satan, prowls around as a roaring lion, just looking for someone to hurt. Resist him, stand firm in the faith, and he will flee from you. We are truly strangers here, but someday soon we'll be going home to heaven."

Affirmation: I will do things that please God!

What A Mighty Hand

Humble yourselves (therefore) under God's mighty hand.   (1 Peter 5:6)

Verse I: Hum - ble your - selves, Hum - ble your - selves, Un - der God's might - y hand. Hum - ble your - selves, Hum - ble your - selves, Un - der God's might - y hand. What a might - y hand!

Chorus: What a mighty hand, a mighty hand has He. What a mighty hand, that calms the raging sea. What a mighty hand, a hand protecting me. What a mighty hand has He.

Second PETER
A SIMPLE REMINDER

2 Peter 3:18 Grow in grace and knowledge of our Lord and Savior Jesus Christ.

Grace

Has anyone ever written you a reminder note? Peter writes his second letter as a friendly reminder note to all believers.

"If we follow Jesus, we will never fail." This is a promise of God!

"So be good Christians having self-control, kindness, and brotherly love. And be faithful to memorize the words spoken by the prophets.   Each day, think about the commands of Jesus Christ. If we do these things, we will grow. We will grow in grace and in the knowledge of our Lord and Savior Jesus Christ."

Affirmation: I will remind someone of God's love for us!

420

Grow in Grace

Grow in grace and knowledge of our Lord and Savior
Jesus Christ. (II Peter 3:18)

Grow in grace and know-ledge of our

Lord and Sav - ior Je - sus Christ.

Grow in grace and know-ledge of our

Lord and Sav - ior Je-sus Christ. Grow

strong in the Lord and love Him to-day.

Grow in grace, grow in grace. Grow

strong in the Lord and love Him to-day.

Grow in grace in the Lord.

421

First JOHN

WALKING WITH GOD

1 John 4:7 Love one another, for love comes from God.

John tells us that if we are to walk with God, we must walk in the light. For God is light. We are to be honest when we speak and loving to those in need. If we walk in the light, Satan, that prince of darkness, can never harm us. John also reminds us that God is love. "Dear children, let us not love with words, but with actions and truth." If we walk in the light and in His love, surely we will walk with Jesus forever in heaven.

That's a mighty promise!

Affirmation: I will walk with Jesus!

Jesus Loves The Little Children

Love one another, for love
comes from God,   (1 John 4:7)

Love one an-oth-er all you child-ren.

Love one an-oth-er in the Lord. Red and

yel - low, black and white, they are

pre - cious in His sight. Child - ren

love one an-oth-er in the Lord.

Verse I: Jesus loves the little children, all the children of the world. Red and yellow, black and white, they are precious in His sight. Jesus loves the little children of the world.

Verse II: Love comes from God, little children. Love them, for love is of the Lord. Red and yellow, black and white, they are precious in His sight. We must love them all for love is of the Lord.

Second JOHN

NEVER TOO YOUNG!

2 John 1:6 This is love, that we walk (in) His commandments.

In John's second letter, he writes to an unnamed woman and her children. John loved children very much ... just like Jesus. John was so happy to learn these children were walking with Jesus. "Love one another," he writes, "and this is love: that we walk according to Jesus' commandments."

Each child is very special. Each of you have a very important work to do in God's kingdom. Remember, you're never too young to love one another.

Affirmation: I will love Jesus!

424

This Is Love

*This is love, that we walk (in) His
commandments. (2 John 1:6)*

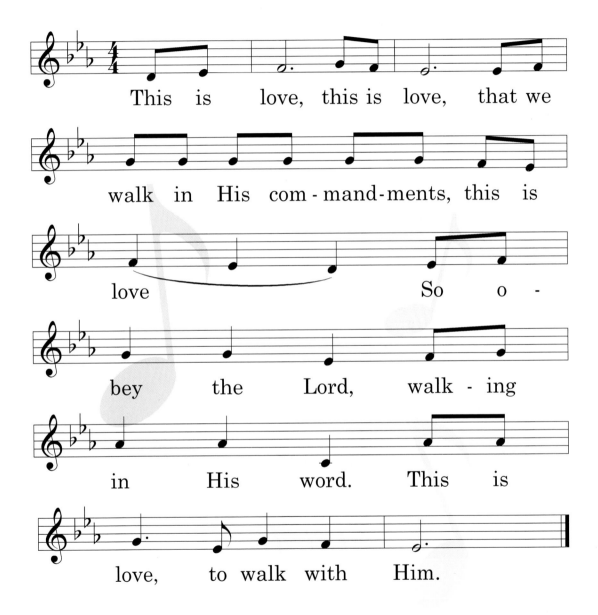

This   is   love,   this   is   love,   that   we

walk   in   His   com - mand - ments,   this   is

love   So   o -

bey   the   Lord,   walk - ing

in   His   word.   This   is

love,   to   walk   with   Him.

Third OHN

I'VE GOT HOSPITALITY

3 John 1:8 We ought to show hospitality (to Christians) so that we may work together for truth.

In John's third letter he writes to his dear Christian friend named Gaius. He says many kind things to Gaius to encourage him. Gaius was living his life in a way that pleased Jesus. Perhaps his greatest gift was that of hospitality. He would always take care of the missionaries who came to visit his church. He made sure they had a warm meal and a place to sleep. We, too, ought to show hospitality to our Christian friends and workers.

Affirmation: I will show my hospitality by saying a kind word to a Christian worker this week.

Show Hospitality

We ought to show hospitality to (Christians) so that
we may work together for truth. (III John 1:8)

Verse I: We ought to show hos-pi-tal-i-ty, mm-

hmm, mm-hmm. We ought to show hos-pi-tal-i-ty, mm-

hmm, mm-hmm. We ought to show hos-pi-tal-i-ty to

those who love the Lord, you see, mm-

hmm, mm-hmm, mm-hmm.

Verse II: We should work together for truth, mm-hmm, mm-hmm. We should work together for truth, mm-hmm, mm-hmm. We should work together for truth, just like Moses, Paul and Ruth, mm-hmm, mm-hmm, mm-hmm.

JUDE   BEWARE!

Jude 1:21 Keep yourselves in the love of God.

Sometimes we must fight for what we believe in. Jude, the other brother of Jesus, warns us in this short letter to beware of godless men and women who secretly slip into our churches. Remember, if anyone denies that Jesus is the Son of God, that person is not teaching the truth.

We stand up for Jesus. We put on the armor of faith and march into battle. Using the sword of the Spirit, we fight the good fight!

For the victory has already been won at Calvary. Therefore keep yourselves in the love of God.

Affirmation: I will stand up for Jesus!

Keep Yourselves
In The Love Of God

Keep yourselves in the love of God. (Jude 1:21)

Keep your - self in the love of God,

e - ven when oth - ers think it odd.

Go with the Lord where He may trod and

keep your - self in the love of God.

Love a lit - tle, love a lit - tle lou - ba - de - da.

Love a lit - tle, love a lit - tle lou - ba - de - da.

Love a lit - tle, love a lit - tle lou - ba - de - da, and

keep your - self in the love of God.

REVELATION
THE LAMB'S BOOK OF LIFE
Revelation 21:27

It's wonderful to know that we serve a living Savior. He is at this very moment preparing our homes in heaven. And one day soon, Jesus will break through the clouds and come back to this earth to claim His children. Satan, that old serpent, will be defeated. Then comes the greatest moment in history when Jesus opens the "Lamb's Book of Life."

If you have asked Jesus to come into your heart, your name will be written in the Lamb's Book of Life.

Just think ... God knows your name, and has heard your prayers. If you've never asked Jesus into your heart, but you want to, just pray this little prayer:

Dear Heavenly Father, I believe that Jesus died on a cross for me, and I believe He rose again and lives today. Please forgive me of all my sins and let Jesus come into my heart. Amen.

Into My Heart

(Invitation)

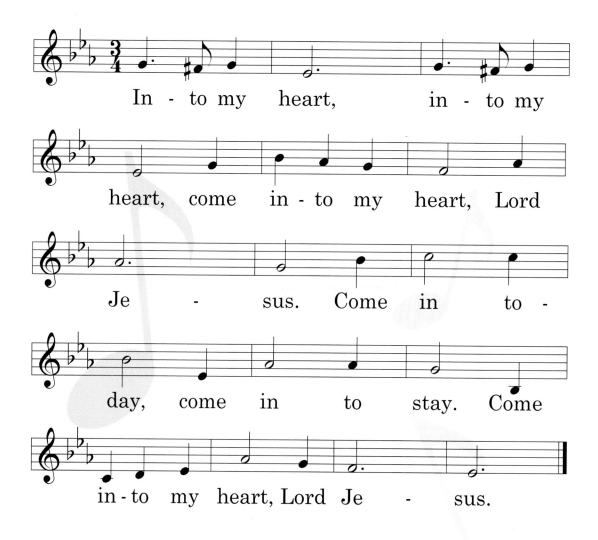

In - to my heart, in - to my heart, come in - to my heart, Lord Je - sus. Come in to - day, come in to stay. Come in - to my heart, Lord Je - sus.

KEY WORD REFERENCE

altar -a place where gifts are brought to God

ambassador -a person selected to bring a special message to others

angel -a messenger sent from heaven

ark -a very big boat, like the one Noah built

Ark of the Covenant -the box used to carry the original copy of the Ten Commandments

armor -a metal covering that protects you

astrology -the study of the stars, moon, sun, and planets

banquet -a special dinner to honor a person or event

baptize -when a Christian is dunked in water as an outward sign of their faith in Jesus

begotten -born into a family

betray -to lie or to tell a secret that you shouldn't

birthright -the honor or blessing given to a first born son

blessing -a prayer or wish for happiness, health, and good fortune

breastplate -a covering worn to protect the chest

caravan -a group of people following each other on a trip

comfort -to help another person when they are sad or sick

covet -to want something that is not yours

crucify -to hang someone on a "T" shaped post until they die

descendant -what you are to your parents and what your parents are to your grandparents

deliverance -to be made safe from danger or harm

disciple -a follower who learns from another person

faith -to believe or trust something even though you cannot see it.

famine -a time when there is little or no food

forbidden -when no one is allowed to have or do a particular thing

forgive -excusing someone who has done something wrong

gallows -the name of the place where people are hanged

gentleness -to be very kind and polite to others

glean -when you gather grain, like wheat, from a field

goodness -being very kind

gospel -good news

grace -when someone gives you something good you didn't work for or deserve

guidance -showing someone how to do something

helmet -a covering to protect the head

holy -something or someone chosen to be very special

hospitality -to treat visitors very nice

humble -not thinking you are better than anyone else

idol -anything that you make more important than God

invisible -something that cannot be seen with your eyes

joy -when you are very happy

judge -to decide what happens to someone or something

kindness -when you are fair and nice

Lamb's Book of Life - a heavenly book containing the names of people who are saved.

locust -an insect that looks like a grasshopper

manger -an open box used to feed animals like horses and cows

manna -a kind of bread God sent from heaven

mercy -to show someone forgiveness

miracle -amazing thing that cannot be explained

missionary -a person who tells others about Jesus

mock -to make fun of or be mean to someone else

mourn -to be very sad when someone dies

noble -when you are very important or have great courage

offering -a gift gladly given

parable -a story that teaches a lesson

patience -being able to wait for something politely

peace -feeling good inside or a time of quiet

perish -to die

pillar -a tall post or column

plague -when a lot of people have the same bad trouble or illness

praise -telling how much you like someone or something

pray -to speak to God

preach -telling a message or news to other people

priest -a person who has a special relationship with God

prison -a place to lock someone inside

proclaim -to make an announcement

prophet -someone God asks to tell others about Him; sometimes God gives a prophet a special message to tell others

protect -to keep safe or keep from getting hurt

pure -something that is perfect with no mistakes

remnant -the part or piece that is left

repent -to say you're sorry and ask forgiveness

rescue -to set free or keep from being hurt

revelation -to make something known that had been hidden

righteous -to do what is right

riot -a group of people who are making a lot of noise and sometimes acting bad

sacrifice -to give away something as a gift

salvation -what God gives to anyone who wants to be a part of his family

savior -someone who saves us from something bad; in the Bible, Jesus is called Savior

scripture -sentences and verses from the Bible

seek -to look for something

Self-control -to be able to keep yourself from getting in trouble

serpent -a reptile, usually a snake

servant -a person who works for someone else

shield -a piece of armor used to protect and keep you safe

slavery -when one person is owned by another person

slingshot -a "Y" shaped stick used to throw rocks or stones

staff -a tall cane or stick someone carries to help them walk

swaddling -strips of cloth wrapped around a newborn baby

sword -a weapon with a sharp blade and a handle

taxes -extra fees or money people have to pay to their government

temple -the special building where people go to worship God

tomb -a grave or place where the dead are buried

victory -when you win

whirlwind -air that turns in very fast circles, like a tornado

wicked -very bad

wise -to be very smart and know a lot of answers

worship -to love and honor